UKULELE
BEGINNER TO BRILLIANT

BOOK 3:
THE BLUES

UKULELE BEGINNER TO BRILLIANT

BOOK 3: THE BLUES

By

Doug Falconer

OTHER BOOKS BY THE AUTHOR:
Ukulele Beginner to Brilliant Book 1: Beginner
Ukulele Beginner to Brilliant Book 2: Intermediate
Ukulele Beginner to Brilliant Book 4: The System (Advanced)
Ukulele Beginner to Brilliant: Collected Edition
How to Improvise on the Baritone Ukulele

As Douglas Robert Falconer:
BURNS: His Life and Times Explored Through Twelve of His Most Famous Songs (Arranged for Ukulele)
BURNS: His Life and Times Explored Through Twelve of His Most Famous Songs (GUITAR EDITION)

All available on Amazon in paperback and eBook format.

Copyright © 2018 Doug Falconer
All rights reserved.
ISBN-13: 9781793846600

DEDICATION

To Sue with love

CONTENTS

Introduction – what is the blues? Video links	1
Exercises	3
Notes on the fretboard	5
PART ONE: BLUES IN THE KEY OF C	7
LESSON 1: The 12 Bar Blues Structure – The C Blues Scale – Improvising	8
LESSON 2: F7 and G7 – The C Blues Scale at the 3rd fret – Improvising	10
LESSON 3: 2 finger blues in C – mixing chords and melody	12
LESSON 4: C7 blues – mixing chords and melody	13
LESSON 5: Major, minor and 7th Blues progressions – Improvising – bends and vibrato	14
LESSON 6: Turnarounds – Improvising	15
LESSON 7: The Blues Shuffle	16
PART TWO: SIX CLASSIC BLUES SONGS (in Keys C F and A)	19
LESSON 8: **Sitting on Top of the World (Key C)** – the Vamp – the Flamenco strum	20
LESSON 9: **When the Saints Go Marching In (Key C)** – improvising – chord melody	22
LESSON 10: **Goin' Down the Road Feelin' Bad (Key F)**	26
LESSON 11: A Method for Transposing songs to another Key – The Nashville and Classical Number Systems Revisited	27
LESSON 12: **Goin' Down the Road Feelin' Bad (Key A)** chord melody – A Blues Scale – A Major Pentatonic Scale - Improvising in A	30
LESSON 13: **Key to the Highway (Key A)** – "licks" mixing major and minor	32
LESSON 14: **Key to the Highway (Key A)** two solo arrangements (fingerpicking and chord melody)	35
LESSON 15: **Sweet Home Chicago (Key A)** – chords, melody and turnarounds in A	36
LESSON 16: **Trouble in Mind (Key A)** – chord melody	38
PART THREE: CALL AND RESPONSE – Blues in Keys of Gm, C, A	41
LESSON 17: Call and Response – Writing a Blues Song – **Baby Please Don't Go (Key Gm)** – chord melody – G Blues Scale – Improvising	42
LESSON 18: Fingerpicking patterns – syncopation – call and response – **The Blues Had a Baby (Key C)**	46
LESSON 19: **You Got to Move (Key Gm)** – fingerpicking and "groove" arrangements	50
LESSON 20: The riff – **Little Red Rooster (Key C)**	54
LESSON 21: **I'm So Glad (Key A)**	57
PART FOUR: TWO MORE CLASSIC BLUES IN C and Dm – THE FIVE BLUES SCALE PATTERNS	59
LESSON 22: **Tin Roof Blues (Key C)** fingerpicking arrangement, using the "layover"	60
LESSON 23: **Saint James Infirmary (Key Dm)** – A7#9 chord – chord melody arrangement – D Blues scales	61
LESSON 24: **Putting it all Together – The Blues Scale (the Five Patterns)**	64
AFTERWORD	66
APPENDIX: The Cycle of Fifths Explained	

ACKNOWLEDGEMENTS

Thanks to Graham Majin for his wonderful cover and lifelong friendship

A Note to the Reader

This book is for readers worldwide but, as someone once said, "you can't please all of the people all of the time". So, I have used UK English spelling throughout rather than American (e.g. "acknowledgement" rather than "acknowledgment").

However, where music terminology is concerned I have used both American and British but given preference to American terms as I believe they are clearer (e.g. quarter note rather than crotchet).

I hope my fairly arbitrary editorial decisions will not upset anyone or affect their pleasure in working with this book.

INTRODUCTION

Welcome to Book 3: THE BLUES.

This book is for the player who can already play a few chords and read TAB. However, I have tried to make it accessible to new players as well because, although it carries on from Books 1 and 2, it is in many ways a "standalone" book on a specific area of music and, in consequence, begins easy before introducing more challenging material.

What is Blues music?

Blues, like Jazz, was born in the early 20th century out of the melting pot of cultures that is America. It was born out of slavery, of black Americans exposed to white European influenced folk music and creating something new, simple and powerful. It exploded in popularity and influence in the 1960's, heavily influencing rock'n'roll music, and being championed by young, successful white musicians like the Rolling Stones and Eric Clapton. They were quick to acknowledge their debt to the black artists that influenced them, many of whom had been living in relative poverty and obscurity, and helped introduce them to a worldwide audience. The original bluesmen were rediscovered: Muddy Waters, Howlin' Wolf, Skip James, Robert Johnson, John Lee Hooker, Lightnin' Hopkins, Mississippi John Hurt, Fred McDowell, B B King and many, many others.

The Blues is a deceptively simple art form, relying on a few ingredients yet capable of great depth and expression:
- Melodies based on a simple scale that blurs the line between major and minor
- a repetitive structure (commonly 12 or 8 bars) involving only three chords
- the **riff** (a repeated phrase or motif) that works like the "hook" in pop music
- improvised solos that involve bending notes
- call and response (also found in spirituals and sea shanties)

Videos to help with the lessons are on my YouTube channel, which you can find by typing, "Ukulele Beginner to Brilliant" into the search box or using this link here:

https://www.youtube.com/channel/UCHY9Vic35cnPiN8uHyaKZcw/playlists

Book 3: The Blues. These videos are here:
https://www.youtube.com/playlist?playnext=1&list=PLzqwFChUowVmZzirg91nVW_G4QTk8m5dh&index=1

If you are a complete beginner you may want to check out my internet course on Book 1 here:

https://www.youtube.com/playlist?list=PLzqwFChUowVl__suqYUKJiTGoBZU9KBKH

Before we get into playing the blues on the ukulele here is a one page reference guide for new players, not wholly familiar with chord boxes, notation for fingering, TAB or music notation. It is a brief summary so if unclear I refer you to Book 1 in this series, where everything is explained in detail. It is then followed by some exercises for both hands.

1. The Chord Box

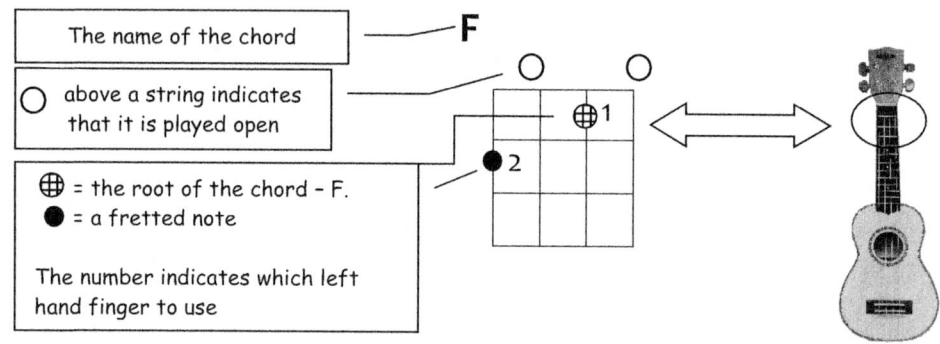

The name of the chord — F

○ above a string indicates that it is played open

⊕ = the root of the chord – F.
● = a fretted note

The number indicates which left hand finger to use

2. The Fingers

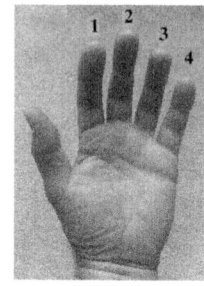

LEFT HAND   RIGHT HAND

3. TAB

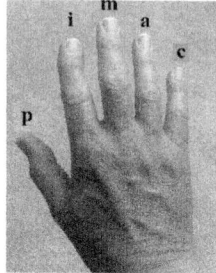

OR

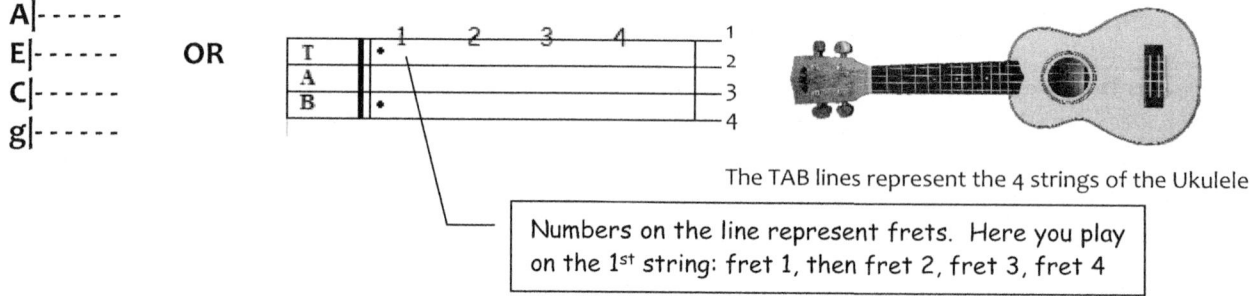

The TAB lines represent the 4 strings of the Ukulele

Numbers on the line represent frets. Here you play on the 1st string: fret 1, then fret 2, fret 3, fret 4

4. Music Notation

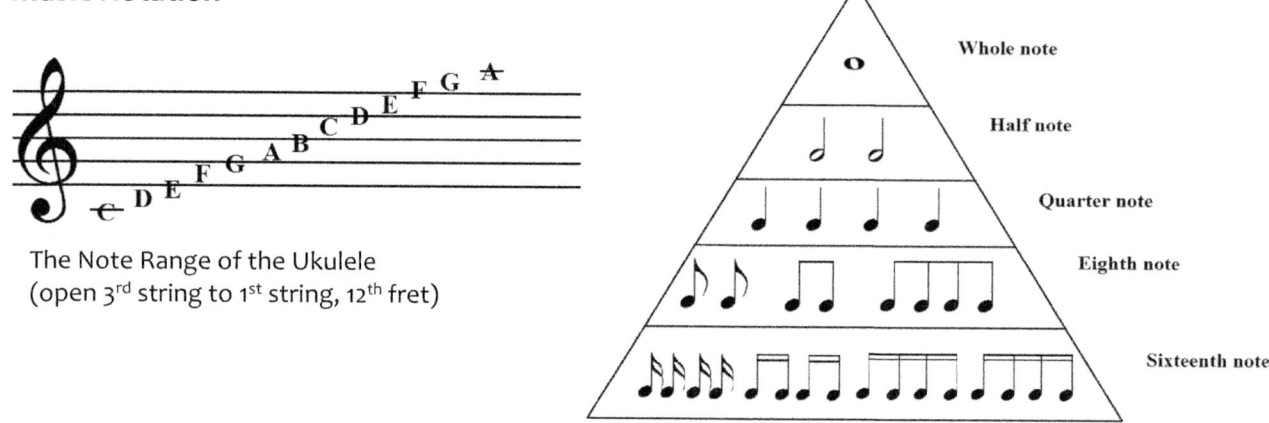

The Note Range of the Ukulele
(open 3rd string to 1st string, 12th fret)

NOTE VALUES

Three Laws of Playing

1. **The Law of Minimum Motion** (the further your fingers stray from the notes the longer it takes to get back to them, your fingers will tire, you will make more mistakes, your playing will be slower)
2. **The Law of Relaxation** (being tense means you can't move and you get tired very easily – go for relaxed flow)
3. **The Law of Slow** (build your muscle memory with slow, short but frequent practice)

Daily/Warmup Exercises

Strength, stamina and flexibility. This is weight training, cardio and yoga for your fingers; without them you will never become a musical athlete. We are lucky because the ukulele has soft nylon strings (as opposed to steel) under low tension so, relative to other string instruments, very little strength is needed to play. However, your fingers still have to be educated to make the correct shapes and movements and that takes practice.

Here are some warmup exercises for both the right hand and the left hand. Spend 5 minutes at the start of your practice doing one or two for each hand.

Left Hand

Exercise 1: Finger Independence

```
A|-1-2-3-4--|-4-3-2-1-|-1-4-3-4-|-2-4-3-4--|
E|----------|---------|---------|----------|
C|----------|---------|---------|----------|
g|----------|---------|---------|----------|
```

Place your L hand 1st finger on the 1st fret; 2nd finger on the 2nd fret; 3rd finger on the 3rd fret, 4th finger on the 4th fret – and keep them there even when not playing a note, just hover (relaxed) above the string (The Law of Minimum Motion).
Use your right hand thumb to pick all notes or practice alternating the i and m fingers (see right hand exercises 1 and 2 below).
Tips: Play <u>slowly</u> and smoothly, focus on <u>minimum movement</u> and <u>relax</u> a finger as soon as it is played.

Exercise 2: Slurs (hammer ons and pull offs)

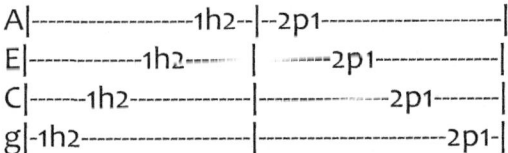

The fingering is as before so the numbers above refer to the left hand finger and also the fret (e.g. finger 2 is on fret 2). Play the 4th string 1st note, 1st fret with your 1st finger, then **hammer on (h)** the 2nd finger to sound the 2nd note (<u>without</u> playing it with your right hand). Do the same on strings 3, 2 and 1. Then, in the next bar play the note on fret 2 and **pull off (p)** the 2nd finger with the 1st finger already holding down fret 1.

Repeat Exercise 2 with the other fingers: 2h3; 3h4; 2h4; 1h4; 1h3. Focus on timing and volume: count 1&, 2&, etc with every beat being of equal length and volume.

Development: you can also try playing triplets which alternate h & p:
Exercise 3:

```
A|------------------------2p1h2--|--1h2p1------------------------|
E|-----------------1h2p1-----------|-----------2p1h2--------------|
C|---------2p1h2-------------------|------------------1h2p1--------|
g|-1h2p1---------------------------|---------------------2p1h2-|
```

Repeat for the other finger combinations: 23, 34, 24, 14, 13

Right Hand

Exercise 1:
Practise slowly but the ultimate aim is for a fast alternation of the index (i) and middle (m) fingers.

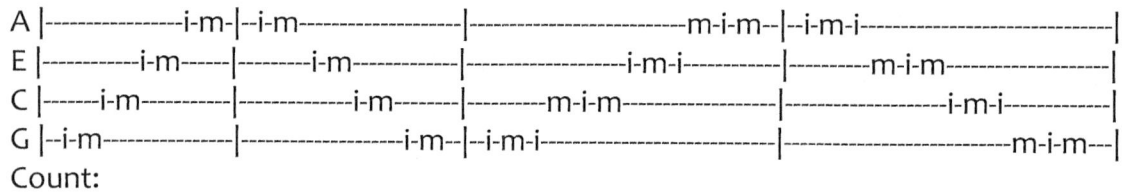

Count:
    1& 2& 3& 4& 1& 2& 3& 4 &   1&a 2&a 3&a 4&a   1&a 2&a 3&a 4&a

Exercise 2:
Building speed
Count:
   1 2 3 4   1 2 3& 4&   1 2 3 4   1 & 2 e & e 3 & 4 e & e

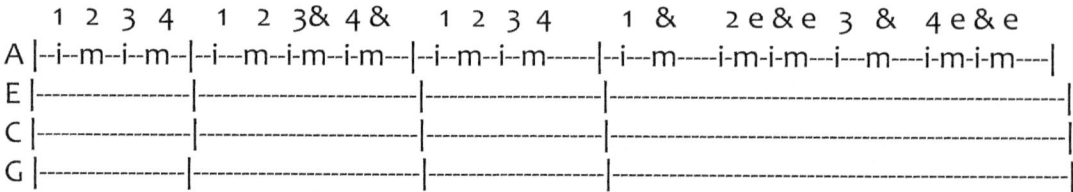

Exercise 3:
Triplets and "Swing" rhythm
Count:
  1 2 3 1 & a 2 & a 3 & a 1 2 3 1 & a 2 & a 3 & a

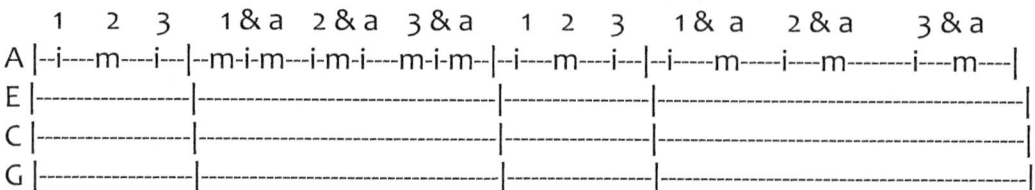

Exercise 4:
This is a fingerpicking pattern with the thumb alternating, on the beat, between the 3rd and 4th strings. For variety, practise it while holding down chords. Use it, as an alternative to strumming, to play any song in 4/4 time.

```
A |------------------m---------------------m----|
E |--------i---------------------i--------------|
C |--p----- --------------p---------------------|
G |-- --------p---------------------p-----------|
   1  &  2  &  3  &  4  &
```

Exercise 5:
Practise any of the strumming patterns you have learned so far. For example, the Triple Strum or the "Boom Chicka" from Book 2 – keep a loose, relaxed wrist.

REFERENCE
THE NOTES ON THE UKULELE FRETBOARD

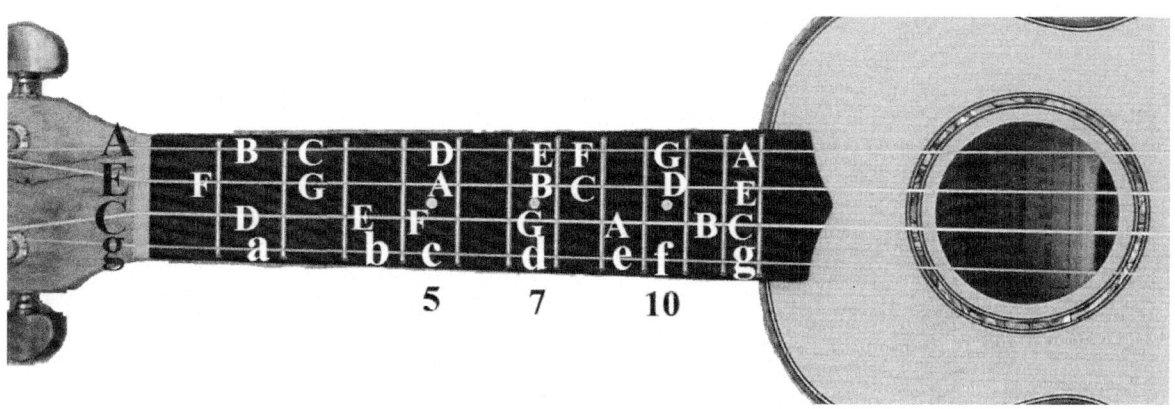

PART ONE
BASIC ELEMENTS OF THE BLUES
(KEY OF C)

12 BAR STRUCTURE
TRIPLETS
THE BLUES SCALE
BENDS AND VIBRATO
TURNAROUNDS

LESSON 1
The 12 Bar Blues Structure - The C Blues Scale - Improvising

1. CHORDS
The I IV and V chords in the Key of C are: C F and G.

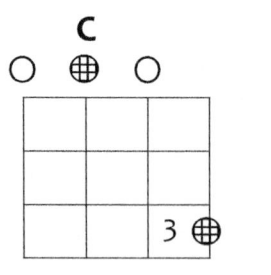 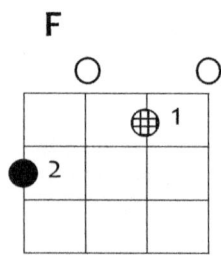 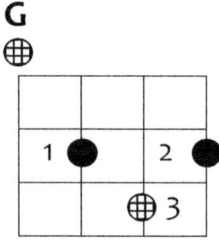

○ = open string   ⊕ = root note

2. THE 12 BAR BLUES STRUCTURE

Virtually the first thing I learned when I started playing guitar was the 12 Bar Blues (every rock and jazz musician knows this chord progression intimately). A basic 12 Bar Blues in the Key of C major looks like this:

C	C or F	C	C
F	F	C	C
G	F	C	G

Note: Playing only the C chord for the first four bars can be a little dull, so sometimes we play F in the second bar for variety.

For each bar count 1 2 3 4 (which is known as 4/4 or Common Time). Use all downstrokes with the right thumb (or first finger). Play slowly and focus on smooth chord changes. Try to memorise the pattern and say each chord either out loud or in your head as you play it.

Practise different strumming patterns:
a) Count 1 2 3 4   (strum D D D D)
b) Count 1 2 3 & 4   (strum D D DU D)
c) Count 1 2 & 3 & 4   (strum D DU DU D)
d) Count 1 2 & 3 & 4 &   (strum D DU DU DU)

3. THE BLUES SCALE (KEY of C) - Preparing to solo

1st finger over 1st fret, 2nd finger over 2nd fret, 3rd finger over 3rd fret. So you play third string open, then 3rd fret with 3rd finger. Move on to 2nd string with 1st finger playing note at 1st fret, 2nd finger playing note at 2nd fret and 3rd finger playing note at 3rd fret. Then 1st string with 1st finger on 1st fret and 3rd finger on 3rd fret.

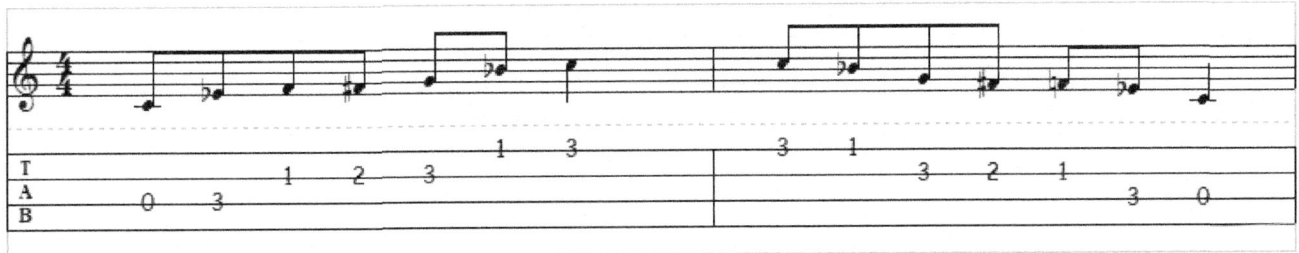

On a fretboard diagram the C blues scale looks like this:

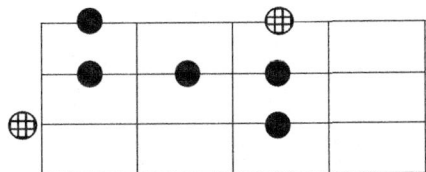

How to use the Blues Scale.

The Blues is a simple structure but, like the ukulele, its simplicity and limitations are a great strength and give infinite freedom of expression. The most interesting thing about the blues harmonically is that it is neither major nor minor. The "blue" note is the flattened third. So, in the key of C major the third is E and the blue note flattens it to Eb. The scale also contains the b5 (Gb) beloved of Bebop Jazz and the b7 note (Bb).

The amazing thing is that the scale will fit over the entire progression whether the chords are major, minor or seventh. In other words, **this one simple scale will fit Blues progressions using the following chords:**
- C F and G (major);
- Cm Fm and Gm (minor);
- C7 F7 and G7 (sevenths)

EAR TRAINING/IMPROVISING
Two methods:

1. Record the 12 bar chord progression and play it back so that you can improvise over the top of it using the blues scale.
2. **Recommended:** this is an excellent way of developing your ear and your timing. Rather than play along to the chord sequence, play alone keeping time with your foot. Start slowly at first. On the first beat of the bar play the chord then improvise for the other beats. So in your head you are thinking and counting: "chord 2 3 4; chord 2 3 4; chord 2 3 4... etc".

Try this:
1. Play the chord on the first beat of every bar but then only play quarter notes (i.e. only play notes on beats 2, 3 and 4).
2. Play the chord on the first beat of every bar but then play only eighth notes (counting: 1 (chord) 2 & 3 & 4 &...)
3. Play the chord on the first beat of every bar, but then play eight notes on beats 2 and 3 and a triplet (three notes) on beat 4.
4. Play the chord on the first beat of every bar, but then improvise freely for the next 3 beats in any way you like.

LESSON 2
Chords of F7 and G7 – The C Blues Scale at the 3rd fret – Improvising

1. Warm up using the exercises from last lesson

2. **CHORDS** – Note the new C shape. The first finger "bars" both the 1st and 2nd string at the 1st fret which takes some practice but develops later into a full bar across all 4 strings which enables you to play chord shapes further up the neck.

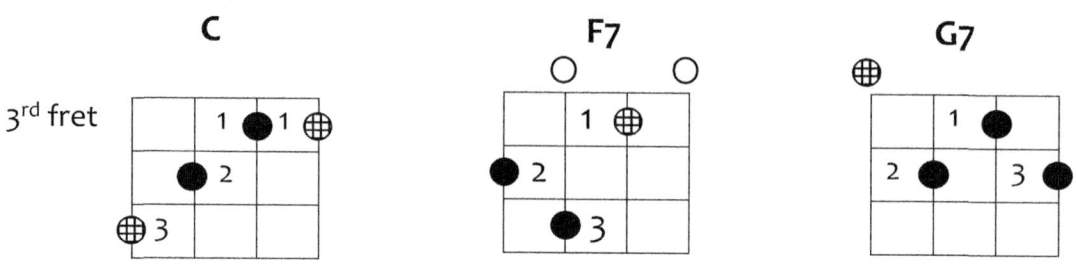

3. The **12 Bar progression** takes the basic chords from Lesson 1, but sounds "bluesier" with the addition of 7th notes to the chords. Practise until the chord changes are fluent and the sequence memorised.

C	F7	C	C
F7	F7	C	C
G7	F7	C	G7

4. **The C Blues Scale** at the 3rd fret. Move all four left hand fingers up the fingerboard so that the 1st finger is now on the 3rd fret (2nd finger on 4th fret; 3rd finger on 5th fret; and 4th finger on 6th fret).

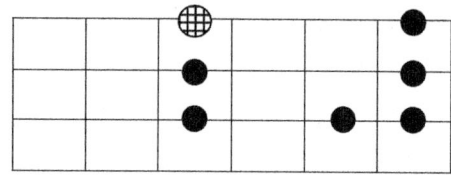

With the C major chord superimposed on top (in triangles) it is easy to see that the scale falls comfortably under the fingers while holding down the chord, making changing from playing single notes to strumming faster and easier:

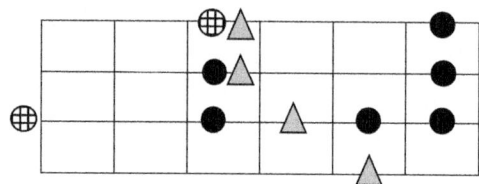

C Blues Scale using triplets:

A common feature of the blues is the use of **triplet** rhythm. So try practising the scale above using **triplets** (the grouped notes with -3- written above).

Use a metronome to keep in strict time and improve your sense of rhythm. E.g. The first bar is counted like this: 1 2&a 3& 4; the second bar is 1&a 2&a 3& 4. A good method for getting the rhythm in your body, before you even pick up your ukulele, is to tap a foot – 4 regular beats and then use your right hand to tap the rhythm above on top of the steady 4 beat.

5. IMPROVISING:

Once you can play the scale fluently, try improvising – first with just the C chord; then with the complete progression. As in the previous lesson, record the whole chord sequence or, practise it solo by playing the chord on the first beat of the bar and then playing quarter notes, then eighth notes, then triplets, then freely.

LESSON 3
2 finger blues in C

1. Warm up using the exercises in Lesson 1.
2. By now you should have memorised this 12 bar sequence of chords and be able to play them, using both versions of the C major chord:

    |C |F7 |C |C |
    |F7 |F7 |C |C |
    |G7 |F7 |C |G7 |

3. **REPERTOIRE:** Here is a piece using the chord progression above; it can be played comfortably with just the right hand thumb and uses only two left hand fingers (1 and 3) to add the melody:

Two Finger Blues

LESSON 4
C7 Blues

1. Warm up using exercises from Lesson 1
2. The Blues, being neither major nor minor and using a flattened 7th in the scale, means that you can substitute C with C7 and still think of yourself as being in the key of C (but with a bluesy sound). Practise the 12 Bar progression from lessons 2 and 3, substituting C7 for C:

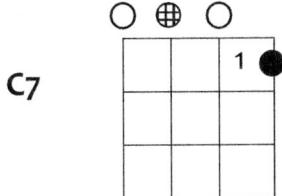

3. **Repertoire**: this next blues still uses only notes from the Blues scale and only two left hand fingers (1 and 3) are required to play the melody. Again, we mix strumming (with thumb of index finger) or pinching and single note picking, using either thumb, index or the alternating i m technique:

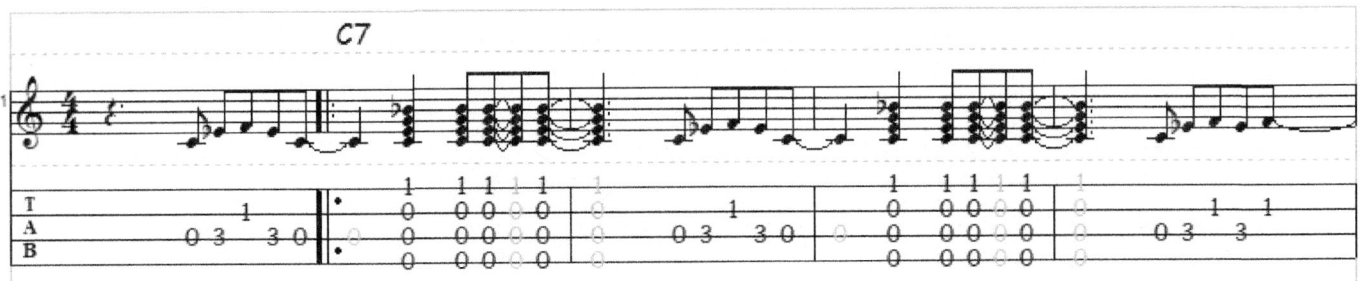

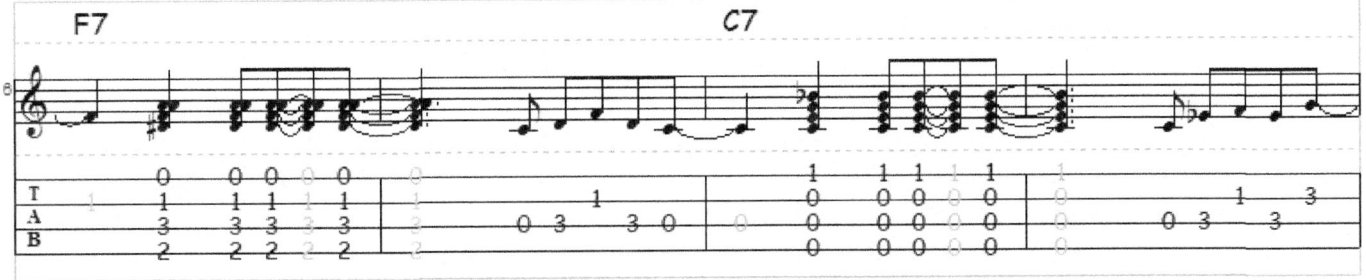

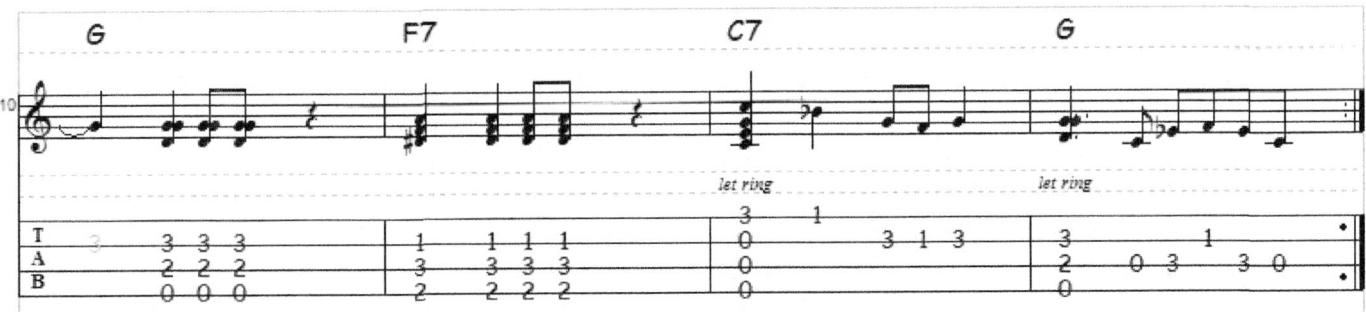

LESSON 5
Major, minor and 7th Blues progressions – Improvising - bends and vibrato

As discussed earlier, because of the nature of the Blues scale (containing a minor 3rd and flat 7th) it works over major, minor and 7th chords. Here is the basic progression using major :

```
|C          |C orF       |C          |C          |
|F          |F           |C          |C          |
|G          |F           |C          |G          |
```

You can also substitute all 7th chords for the chords above;

```
|C7         |C7 orF7     |C7         |C7         |
|F7         |F7          |C7         |C7         |
|G7         |F7          |C7         |G7         |
```

or all minor chords (or minor 7th chords).

```
|Cm         |Cm orFm     |Cm         |Cm         |
|Fm         |Fm          |Cm         |Cm         |
|Gm         |Fm          |Cm         |Gm         |
```

Ear Training

Record all three versions or play solo using the method introduced in Lesson 2, and improvise using the **C blues scale** in both positions.

Advanced Techniques: make the Blues sing!

Blues guitarists would try to make their instrument cry and moan like a human voice. Two ways they achieved this are by: (a) bending notes; (b) vibrato.

Bending notes: this is a key feature of the blues and, although, the ukulele is not as well suited to this technique as the guitar, it is still doable, especially with the 2nd blues scale starting at the 3rd fret (the further from the nut, the easier it gets to bend the notes). You will probably find that the most effective notes to bend are the Bb on the 2nd string 6th fret; the F on the 3rd string 5th fret; and the Eb on the 1st string, 6th fret.

Method: place fingers 1, 2 and 3 on the 3rd string, frets 3, 4 and 5. To bend the F note (3rd string, 5th fret) all you do is play the note then push your 3rd finger up towards the sky, using your other two fingers, placed on the frets below, to help you push. Similarly, bend the 2nd string, 6th fret with your 4th finger by adding your other fingers on the frets below to help push the string up. The effect is that the pitch rises, and then when you "release" allow the string to return

Vibrato: is simply bending the string up and down quickly.
Method 1: bend as before and release, repeat several times rapidly.

Method 2: place your 1st finger on the note you want to use vibrato on and pivot your whole hand downwards then upwards rapidly, using your 1st finger knuckle joint braced against the bottom of the neck. Hard to describe, but this is a favourite technique of guitarist Eric Clapton and you will see him do it in just about any video that features him.

LESSON 6
Turnarounds

Exercise 1:
We are now going to add a "turnaround" which is a widely used way to add some interest to the last 2 bars of any blues progression and take you back to the beginning of the song. Note that the turnaround below also uses **triplets** which you should be familiar with from practising the blues scale in Lesson 2.

Performance notes:
Left hand: on the first beat, the 3rd finger is on the 3rd fret, 1st string. Next, slide it up to the 7th fret. Add the 2nd finger on the 7th fret 3rd string, to play the first triplet. You then move both the 3rd and 2nd fingers down one fret to play the next triplet. Move down 1 fret again to play the final triplet.
Right hand: either play the triplets with i and m; i and a; or thumb and i – whichever is most comfortable.

Exercise 2:
If you find the triplets too difficult, or just want to vary the turnaround slightly then here is a variant where you can either "pinch" the chords or strum them.

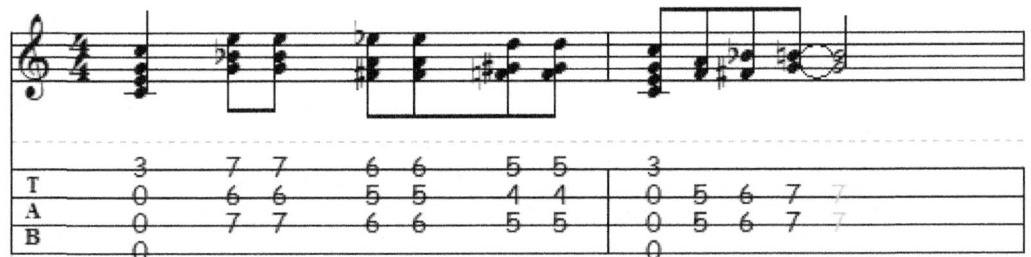

Note: in the first bar you are playing the G7 chord shape but shifting it up to the 7th fret, then 6th, then 5th. You can use up and down strokes of the 1st finger but for the final double notes in the 2nd bar either pinch with i and m or with p and i.

Important rhythmic note: *although the descending G7 shape chords are written as eighth notes, they will "swing" better played as triplets: e.g. Count 2-&-a; 3-&-a... but play on the "2" and on the "-a-".*

Exercise 3:
EAR TRAINING:
Improvise a solo over the 12 Bar Blues chord progression using the C Blues Scale in both positions so far using the guidelines in Lesson 1) and try substituting a turnaround for the last 2 bars.

LESSON 7
The Blues Shuffle

This way of playing has been used in thousands of rock songs and is great for playing with other ukulele players or guitarists. I don't know where the "Blues Shuffle" came from but when I was growing up in the 1970's every guitarist played it and it was the most used rhythm in jam sessions and heard in almost every rock song.

While one guitarist would play full chords, another could add a different texture by playing the shuffle on just two strings (these would be the 6th, 5th and sometimes 4th strings on guitar but we have to adapt the idea for our re-entrant ukuleles):

The 2 string Blues Shuffle

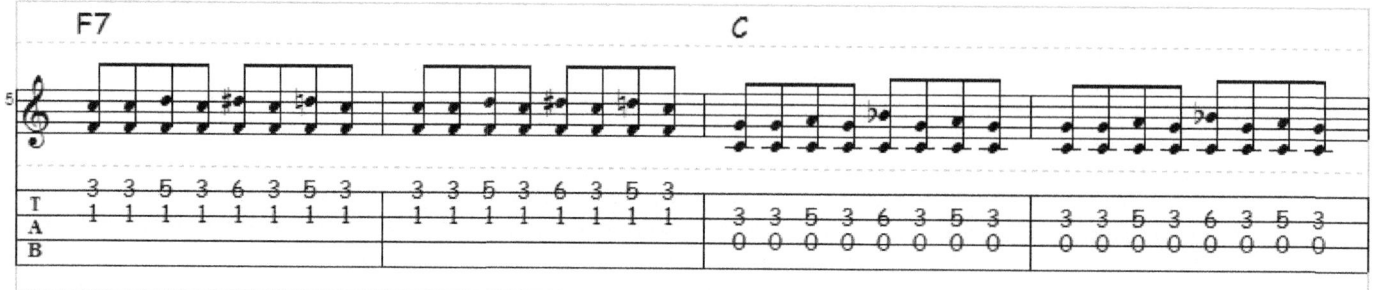

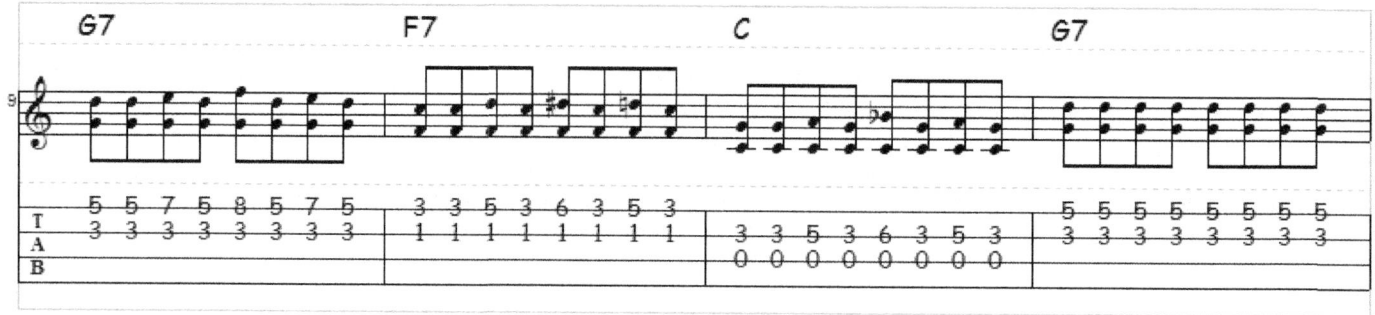

Here is a version playing full chords and using the 4th string to provide the "shuffle" - the moving notes are the same as the previous version but this time used to add interest to the basic C F and G chords. In both shuffles you can also play your turnarounds from Lesson 6 in the last two bars.

The Full Chord Blues Shuffle

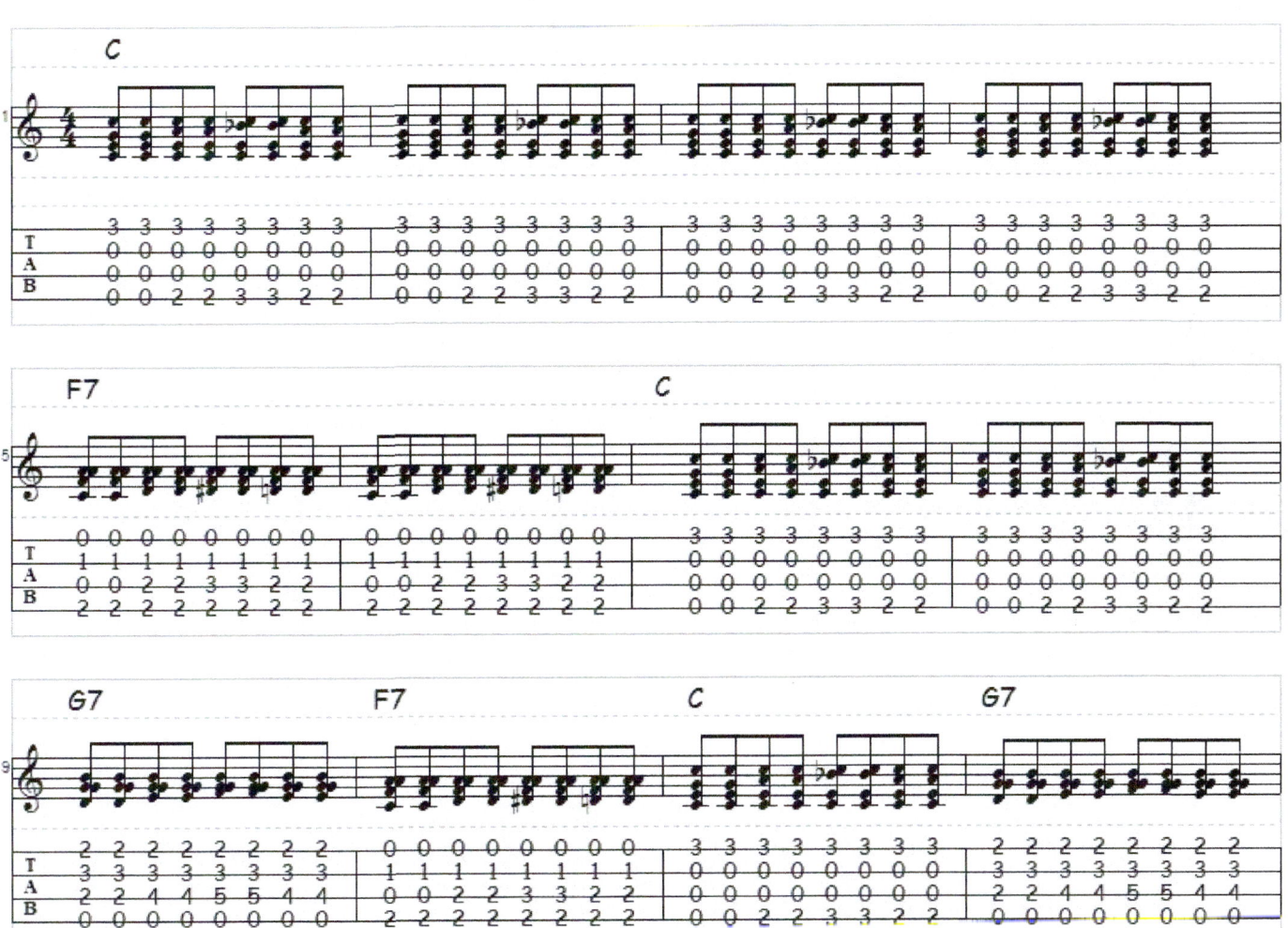

PART TWO

SIX CLASSIC BLUES SONGS
(KEYS C F & A)

LESSON 8
Sitting on Top of the World – the Vamp – the Flamenco strum

A vamp is a short, repeated piece of music. It's the kind of thing you hear behind a singer when he introduces the band or talks to the audience. While the singer talks the band can just groove along nicely in the background. Here is a vamp that we will use in a classic blues song. We play it at the beginning and at the end of every chorus, where we can repeat it as long as we feel like until we are ready to go into the next verse.

This vamp is built around a C5 chord – (so called C5 because it has no third but doubles up on the C root note and the 5th (G). The lack of a 3rd gives it an unusual, ambiguous sound which fits the blues perfectly. (In rock music guitarists often play what are called "power chords" on the low strings, consisting of just the root and the 5th).

To complete our vamp, we add a flat 7th (Bb) to the second chord and a 6th (the note A) to the third chord:

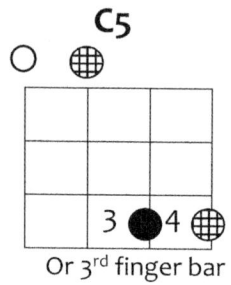
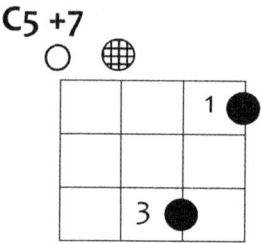
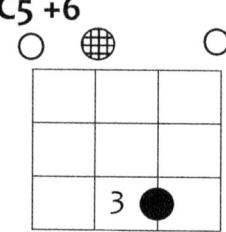

Or 3rd finger bar

Repeated vamp

| C5 | C5 +7 | C5 +6 | C5 +7 | x4 (or more!)

Practise the vamp until you are ready to go on to the song.

Sitting on Top of the World (4/4)

Intro (vamp): | C5 | C5 +7 | C5 +6 | C5 +7 | x4

T' was in the [C5] Spring, one sunny [C5+7] day
My sweetheart [F7] left me, she went [C5] away

Chorus: But now she's gone and I don't [G7] worry
Cause I' m [F7] sitting on top of the [C5 vamp] world

She called me up from El Paso,
Said to me, "Darling, I miss you so."

Repeat Chorus

Ashes to ashes, dust to dust,
Show me a woman a man can trust

Repeat Chorus

Don't like my peaches, don't shake my tree
Get out my orchard, let my peaches be

Repeat Chorus

Advanced Technique: the rasqueado/flamenco strum
This is a technique I've borrowed from flamenco guitar and I use it a lot on the ukulele.

You can add rhythmic impact to the C5 vamp by using this on the second beat of the bar. It might take a month or two to master but it is well worth it.

Method: You flick the right hand fingers out in this order: c (pinkie), a, m, i so that the half beat is divided into 3 with the index finger downstroke on the next main beat. Probably easier to understand in a diagram; it is counted like this in the vamp:

1	&	2	&	3	&	4	&
D (i)	D (cam)	D i	u (i)		u (i)	D (i)	u (i)

D for downstroke; u for upstroke

Note: the **rasqueado** starts on the '&' with the pinkie and then the a m and i fingers all following smoothly so that the i finger's downstroke is timed to hit beat 2. So the count is: **"1   &-e-a   2"**

To create a little bit showbiz razzamatazz, as you perform the rasgueado you can move your right hand in a clockwise circle, George Formby fan stroke style. There is also a video of Lightnin' Hopkins on YouTube, performing **Baby, Please Don't Go** where he is strumming but does a neat, little circle thing with his right hand which just looks cool. For the same reason, guitarists like Pete Townshend do the "windmill thing" with their arms. They could just strum the chord, but a little flashy showing off always goes down well in public.

LESSON 9
When the Saints Go Marching In

Many early twentieth century songs are hard to categorise clearly as either folk, country, jazz or blues because musicians from different backgrounds shared ideas and influenced each other. Early folk, country, jazz and blues have much in common and I think you could label this next song Blues or Jazz. Here is the lead sheet, to add to your strum and sing repertoire:

When the Saints Go Marching In (4/4)

```
|C     |C     |C     |C     |
|C     |C     |G7    |G7    |
|C     |C7    |F     |F     |
|C     |G7    |C     |C     |
```

Oh, when the [C] saints go marching in
Oh, when the saints go marching [G7] in
Lord how I [C] want to be [C7] in that [F] number
When the [C] saints go [G7] marching [C] in

And when the sun begins to shine
And when the sun begins to shine
Lord, how I want to be in that number
When the sun begins to shine

Oh, when the trumpet sounds its call
Oh, when the trumpet sounds its call
Lord, how I want to be in that number
When the trumpet sounds its call

Note: I sometimes play Fm in bar 12 (so you have one bar of F, then after singing "number" you play Fm).

When the Saints Go Marching In (melody)

Analysis:
the melody is very simple, containing only the notes: C, D, E, F, and G (all notes from the C major scale). The D note only appears in the 2 bars (out of 16 bars) where there is a G7 chord (D is the 5th of the G7 chord). So, apart from that, the catchy, engaging melody is made out of only 4 notes: C E F and G.

There is a powerful lesson here for both songwriting and improvising:
you only need a few notes to create a memorable tune.

It is an argument I will go into, in detail, in Book 4 but for now the point I want to make is that making good music is not about ripping up and down scales like a lead guitarist in a rock band (well, not just about that). Impressive though that can be, my point is: if you can't make good music with 4 or 5 notes, then having more notes won't help you. Eric Clapton put it this way: "My driving philosophy about making music is that you can reduce it all down to one note if that note is played with the right kind of sincerity."
(https://www.inspiringquotes.us/quotes/8FrG_C3cGmgOH)

Ear Training

Record the chord progression – if you don't have a recording device then just use your mobile phone (many of my YouTube videos were recorded on my ancient iPhone 4: e.g. Ode to Joy - https://www.youtube.com/watch?v=i84U215wxvM ; and Jake Bugg recorded "Fire" on his iPhone: https://www.youtube.com/watch?v=2rkvcB8kSiM).

There are also various apps and software (like iReal) which provide backing tracks.

Whatever method you use to record the chord backing, try improvising using the following suggestions:

Tips for Improvising

1. Learn the melody first, to the point where you can play it without looking at the music. Don't move on to the next step until you can do this.

2. Improvise by restricting yourself to playing only the arpeggios (the notes of the chords played individually) over the chord changes (C major = C E G; F major = F A C; G7 = G B D F). Only move on when you can do this.

3. Improvise by restricting yourself to playing only the notes that appear in the melody: C E F and G. When the G7 chord comes, use the D note (3rd string; 2nd fret) and the F note (2nd string, 1st fret): emphasise them by playing a phrase that begins &/or ends on either the D or the F note.

4. Use the C major scale but restrict your rhythm so that you only play quarter notes (you can vary this in other ways: e.g. by playing three quarter notes and then a triplet on the 4th beat; or by playing two quarter notes and then eighth notes on the 3rd and 4th beats – so you get 1 2 3& 4&)

5. Use the C blues scale (as 4 above)

6. Improvise freely

When the Saints (Chord Melody)

LESSON 10
Goin' Down the Road Feelin' Bad (Key of F)

Goin' Down the Road Feelin' Bad – is another old song which resists categorisation. It has been covered by country artists like Johnny Cash, by folk musicians on the BBC's Transatlantic Sessions series, by rock group The Grateful Dead, and more recently, by bluesmen John Meyer and Eric Bibb. Like most old songs there are variations in the lyrics and melody but here are my favourite verses. The melody is the same for both verse and chorus and the song usually follows this structure: chorus, verse, chorus, verse, chorus... etc

Goin' Down the Road Feelin' Bad (4/4)

F	F	F	F
Bb	Bb	F	F
Bb	Bb	F	F
C7	C7	F	F

Chorus: [F] Goin' down the road feelin' bad
[Bb] Goin' down the road feelin' [F] bad
[Bb] Goin' down the road feelin' [F] bad
And I [C7] ain't gonna be treated this [F] way

Verses:
Goin' where the water tastes like wine.
Goin' where the water tastes like wine.
Goin' where the water tastes like wine.
Cause this water round here tastes like turpentine

They feed me on cornbread and beans x3
And I ain't gonna be treated this way

Goin' where the chilly winds don't blow x3
And I ain't gonna be treated this way

I'm tired of lyin' in this jail x3
And I ain't gonna be treated this way

Note: the melody is notated in the next lesson

LESSON 11
A method for Transposing songs to another Key

The Nashville and Classical Number Systems Revisited

If you don't know what "The Nashville Number and Classical Number Systems" are, then I refer you back to Book 2, Lesson 10 which explains them. Here is a brief recap. The following chart contains the "secret" to all Western music as it shows the major scales and their notes and chords.

Reference Chart (all Keys)

# or b	I = MAJ	ii = min	iii min	IV = MAJ	V = MAJ	Vi = min	Vii = dim
None	C	D	E	F	G	A	B
# (f)	G	A	B	C	D	E	F#
## (f c)	D	E	F#	G	A	B	C#
### (f c g)	A	B	C#	D	E	F#	G#
#### (f c g d)	E	F#	G#	A	B	C#	D#
##### (f c g d a)	B	C#	D#	E	F#	G#	A#
###### (f c g d a e)	F#	G#	A#	B	C#	D#	E#
b (b)	F	G	A	Bb	C	D	E
b b (b e)	Bb	C	D	Eb	F	G	A
b b b (b e a)	Eb	F	G	Ab	Bb	C	D
b b b b (b e a d)	Ab	Bb	C	Db	Eb	F	G
b b b b b (b e a d g)	Db	Eb	F	Gb	Ab	Bb	C

Explanation: The "Nashville Number System" is, in a nutshell, writing the names of chords down as Arabic numerals (1, 2, 3, etc...). The Classical system (shown in the top line of the table above) is very similar, but uses Roman numerals instead – capitals for major chords and lower case for minor. For example, all the chords in the Key of C are built on the C major scale (the notes: C D E F G A B). So the C chord is I. The D chord is ii, etc... With reference to the table above, if we look at the first and second rows together, the 1st column tells us how many sharps or flats there are in the key ("none" in C major). The rest of the columns use Roman numerals to tell us what degree of the C major scale we are on and what chord is built from it. So, the 4th column tells us we have the iii/3rd degree of the scale which is the note E and that always makes a minor chord = E minor. The I, IV and V columns are highlighted in green because they are the Major chords and the vi (blue) column is the relative minor of the Key. So, the Key is either C major or A minor.

We are now going to **transpose** a melody from the **Key of F major** to the **Key of A major**. The same method can be used to transpose from any key to any other key.

Here is the melody and chords for **Goin' Down the Road Feelin' Bad** in the Key of F major:

Goin' Down the Road Feelin' Bad (melody in F)

How to transpose

Use the Nashville system to write out the chords above the bars. If you refer to the Key signature (one flat: Bb) and the first chord then you can tell that we are in the Key of F major.

Step 1:
Write out the notes in the key, and number them in ascending order, starting on the root:

1	2	3	4	5	6	7
F	G	A	Bb	C	D	E

Step 2:
Write out the chords (using Roman numerals) above the bars (F is the I chord, Bb is the IV chord and C7 is the V7 chord), for example:

```
I               IV    I
|  |  |  |  |  |  |  |  | etc…
```

Step 3:
Write out the melody notes using the numbers in Step 1 (if, as in this case, some of the notes fall below the 1 note or, the 1 note appears an octave higher as the 8 note, then write the numbers on a lower or higher line to show that they are in a different octave:

5|3 5 5|6 5 1|3 | 3 2|

Once you have completed the three steps above, you have a written code that can be transferred to any key. We are now going to look at the song, transposed from F, into the Key of A major (a popular key with guitarists and therefore a popular key in folk, country, blues and rock music, as guitar is the main instrument). So, if we look at the Key of A in the Reference chart above then we have:

1	2	3	4	5	6	7
A	B	C#	D	E	F#	G#

So, the I, IV, V (or 1 4 and 5) chords are A D and E and you simply translate the numbers for the melody into the notes above, so 5 becomes the note E, 3 becomes the note C# and so on. It takes time but, like everything else, it becomes quicker and easier with practice.

LESSON 12
Goin' Down the Road Feelin' Bad (Key of A)

[A] Goin' down the road feelin' bad
[D] Goin' down the road feelin' [A] bad
[D] Goin' down the road feelin' [A] bad
And I [E7] ain't gonna be treated this [A]way

Verses:
Goin' where the water tastes like wine x3
Cause this water round here tastes like turpentine

They feed me on cornbread and beans x3
And I ain't gonna be treated this way

Goin' where the chilly winds don't blow x3
And I ain't gonna be treated this way

I'm tired of lyin' in this jail x3
And I ain't gonna be treated this way

Chord Melody arrangement in the Key of A

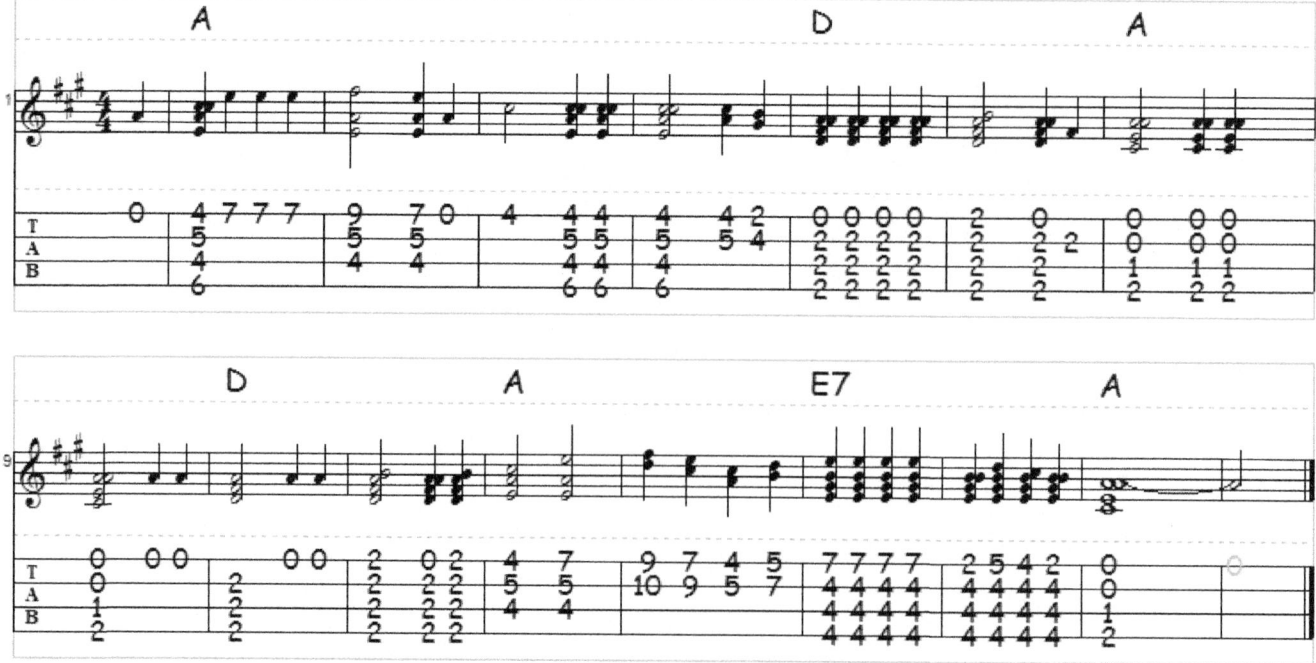

Improvising

To improvise over **Goin' Down the Road** we can use either the **A Blues Scale** for a more "bluesy" sound, or the **A major pentatonic scale** for a more "country" feel (Pentatonics will be explored in more depth in Book 4). Record a backing track and experiment by playing over it using both scales.

A Blues Scale (Notes: A C D D# E G)

Here are two patterns you can use (at the nut and at the 5th fret)

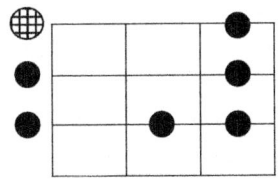
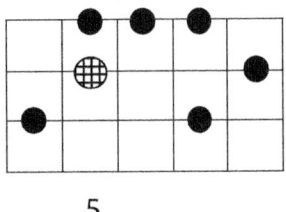

5

Make up your own practice patterns beginning and ending on the root note (as below):

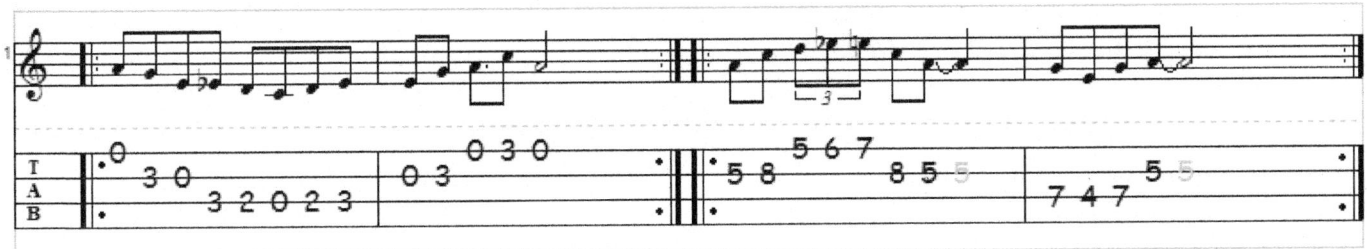

A Major Pentatonic Scale (Notes: 1 2 3 5 6: A B C# E F#)

Here is a pattern with the root on the 2nd string 5th fret.

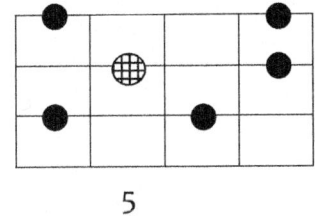

5

LESSON 13

Key to the Highway (Blues in A) – *mixing major and minor*

Here is another classic Blues in the Key of A (the same key that Eric Clapton plays it in. On YouTube you can find an earlier version by Big Bill Broonzy in the Key of E, which you can also play along with if you transpose the key from A to E (using the method shown in Lesson 11).

This is an 8 bar blues (count 4 beats to the bar):

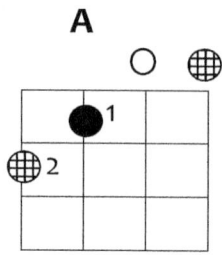 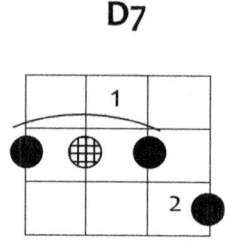 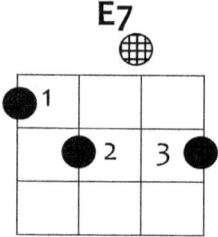

Key to the Highway (4/4)

| A | E7 | D7 | D7 |
| A | E7 | A | E7 |

I got the [A] key to the [E7] highway, I'm [D7] booked out and bound to go,
I'm gonna [A] leave here [E7] running, ain't coming back no [A] more [E7]

I'm going back to the border, where I'm better known,
I'm gonna ride this old highway, ain't coming back no more

Give me one more kiss, mama, just before I go,
I'm gonna leave here running, ain't coming back no more

Now, when the moon peeks over the mountain, You know I'll be on my way
I'm gonna walk, walk this ol' highway, deep until the break of day

So long and good-bye, yes, I had to say good-bye,
'Cause I'm gonna walk, walk this ol' highway, deep 'til the day I die

Key to the Highway (melody)

Analysis:

Last lesson we used the A Blues scale and the A major scale. A distinguishing feature of many blues songs is that they blur the distinction between major and minor. In the melody for Key to the Highway we see both the major third of the chord A - the note C# - and the minor 3rd note, C natural.

If we look at the degrees of the A major scale we have:

        1   2   3   4   5   6   7
        A   B C# D   E   F# G#

But in the song we have:

        1   2 **b3** 3   4   5   6   7
        A   B   **C**   C# D   E   F# G#

Which gives us a kind of hybrid scale with both the major third (C#) and the flattened ("blue") third (C).

We could practice it as a scale like this:

But a more meaningful way is to impose limitations and see how the major and minor 3rd note are used in solos, using short **"licks"**. Try the following exercises:

MIXING MAJOR AND MINOR

Exercise 1:

Note: here we are using the C (the minor 3rd) and emphasising it by playing it on the 1st beat of both bars. We can use this lick with an A major chord, A minor chord or an A7 chord. In the Key of A when we go to the IV chord (D) the riff still works because the C note is the 7th of D and, of course, 7ths sound very bluesy too. It will also work on the V7 chord (E7) but the A note sounds a little out of place and it would be better to add a B note immediately after (as B is the 5th of the E7 chord).

Exercise 2:

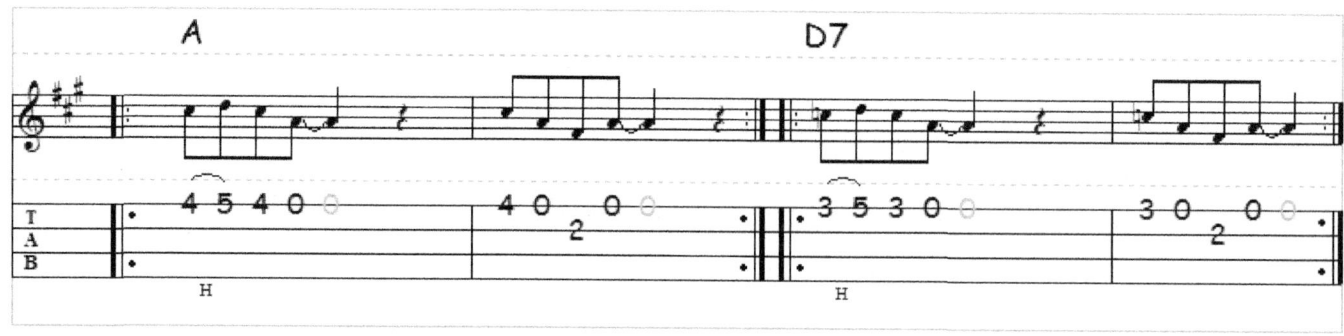

Note: Often in Blues the IV chord is played as a IV7, which doesn't, according to the strict rules of Western harmony, fit the key. In the example above D7 would normally suggest the key of G, not A. Also, if we play the major 3rd (C#) as we do in the lick on the A chord and try to repeat it over the D7 chord then it clashes with the 7th of the D7 chord which is C. So, here we play the same lick but just modify it by dropping the major 3rd to a minor 3rd, which gives that bluesy 7th sound.

Improvising

Record the **Key to the Highway** progression and play with the ideas above. Limiting yourself to the notes in Exercises 1 and 2 will give you more than enough material to construct solos and develop your ear. You could also play along to a recording of the song on YouTube (Eric Clapton performs it in A; Big Bill Broonzy in E).

LESSON 14
Key to the Highway - Fingerpicking

Fingerpicking chords is a pleasing alternative to strumming when accompanying singing. Try playing the following right hand pattern:

We can then apply the same pattern using the chords for **Key to the Highway** (note the alternating thumb):

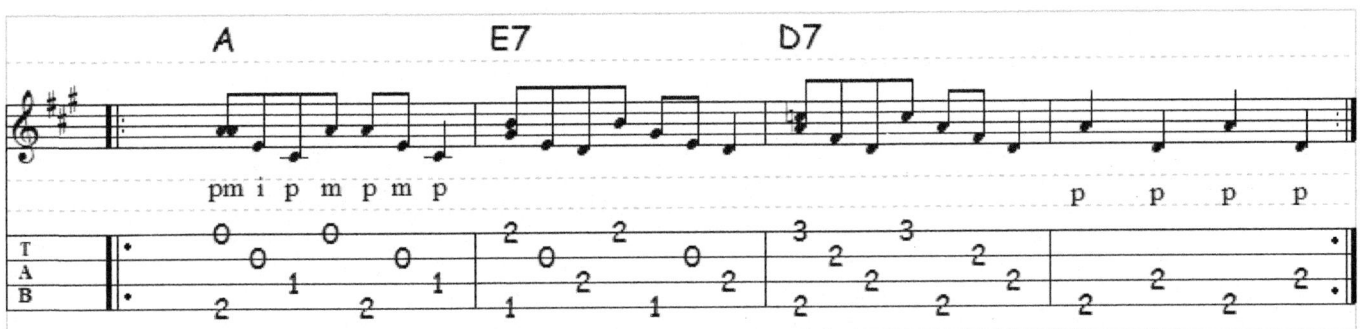

Finally, here is a chord melody version of the song, using a similar fingerpicking pattern to incorporate the melody notes. As before, the thumb alternating between the 4th and 3rd strings is a key ingredient:

Key to the Highway (Chord melody)

LESSON 15
Sweet Home Chicago (Key of A)

Now for a 12 bar classic, often attributed to Robert Johnson ("King of the Delta Blues") – whether or not he wrote it, he certainly made it famous.

Sweet Home Chicago (4/4)

Come [A] on, [D7] baby, don't you want to [A] go.
Come [D7] on, baby, don't you want to [A7] go.
Back to the [E7] land of California – [D7] sweet home Chica- [A] go [E7]

Now [A] one and one is two, [A] two and two is four,
[A] I'm heavy loaded, baby, I'm [A] booked I got to go.

Cryin',[D7] baby, honey, don't you want to [A7] go?
Back to the [E7] land of California, to my [D7] sweet home Chica [A7] go.
[E7]

Now, two and two is four, four and two is six,
You gon' keep on monkeyin' 'round here friend-boy
you gon' get your business in a trick, but I'm cryin'

Baby, honey, don't you want to go?
Back to the land of California, to my sweet home Chicago.

Now, six and two is eight, eight and two is ten,
Friend-boy she trick you one time, she sure gon' do it again

But I'm cryin', hey, hey, baby, don't you want to go?
To the land of California, to my sweet home Chicago.

Come on, baby, don't you want to go?
Come on, baby, don't you want to go?
Back to the land of California, to my sweet home Chicago.

Sweet Home Chicago (melody and turnarounds)

Notes:
- The melody would drop to a low A in the final bar (the "go" of "Chicago") but, owing to the range of the ukulele, it is shown here an octave higher.
- The 2nd, 3rd and 4th repeat bars show three variations on a typical "turnaround" in the Key of A. You can use the same turnarounds in Key to the Highway or any other blues in A for that matter.
- To turn the above into a chord melody, in the 2nd bar you may find it better to play the A note on the 2nd string, 5th fret, rather than use the open 1st string.
- Also, if adapting the melody above to make a chord melody arrangement, you might find it easier to use this D7 shape:

LESSON 16
Trouble in Mind

For the final blues in the Key of A here is a slow 8 bar blues. There is a great rendition by Marianne Faithful, but this ukulele version pays homage to the recording by Lightnin' Hopkins.

Trouble in Mind (4/4)

Intro: A - E7 - A - E7

| A | E7 | A | D7 |
| A | E7 | A | E7 |

Trouble in [A] mind, I'm [E7] blue, but I [A] won't be blue al- [D7]ways,
'cause the [A] sun's gonna [E7] shine round my back door some - [A] day. [E7}

I'm going down to the river, I'm gonna take me a rocking chair,
and if the blues don't leave, I'll rock on away from here.

Trouble in mind, I'm blue, but I won't be blue always,
'cause the sun's gonna shine in my back door someday.

Trouble in mind, that's true, I have almost lost my mind,
life ain't worth living, I feel like I could die.

Trouble in mind, I'm blue, my poor heart is healing slow,
I never had such trouble in my whole life before.

I'm gonna lay my head on some lonesome railroad line,
and let that 2:19 special ease my troubled mind.

Trouble in mind, I'm blue, but I won't be blue always,
'cause the sun's gonna shine in my back door someday.

Trouble in Mind (chord melody)

Performance Notes: this sounds good if you slide into the double notes. For example, at the beginning of Bar 2, place your 2nd and 3rd fingers on the 2nd fret, pluck both notes and slide up into the notes on fret 4. Then, at the end of bar 3 you can pluck fret 2 and slide all the way up to fret 7.

PART THREE

CALL AND RESPONSE

KEY OF G MINOR

Lesson 17
Call and Response – Writing a Blues Song

In the 1930's, a gentleman called Alan Lomax travelled with his father around the American Deep South recording folk music. (you can read about him here: https://www.loc.gov/folklife/lomax/ and find the recordings he made on YouTube). Lomax recorded early blues artists, plantation workers and even prisoners on *chain gangs* (prisoners had to do hard labour such as building roads and to prevent them escaping they were chained together by the ankles). One feature of the plantation and work group songs is **call and response**: a phrase is sung by a lone singer and then the rest of the gang sing a response. Here is an example of a chain gang song called "Lightning Long John": https://www.youtube.com/watch?v=4G5KtQynWvc

Here is another short video where two blues musicians discuss the importance of **call and response** to the blues: https://www.youtube.com/watch?v=P5FhIUKSdU4

In this section we will look at some examples of **Call and Response** in blues songs and how to use it in writing your own songs. But first, here is what Wikipedia has to say (from: https://en.wikipedia.org/wiki/Call_and_response_(music)):

Leader/chorus call and response
A single leader makes a musical statement, and then the chorus responds together. American bluesman Muddy Waters utilizes call and response in one of his signature songs, **Mannish Boy** which is almost entirely leader/chorus call and response (https://www.youtube.com/watch?v=w5IOou6qN1o)

CALL: Waters' vocal: "Now when I was a young boy"
RESPONSE: (Harmonica/rhythm section riff)
CALL: Waters: "At the age of 5"
RESPONSE: (Harmonica/rhythm section riff)

Another great example is from Chuck Berry's **School Day (Ring Ring Goes the Bell)**
(**https://www.youtube.com/watch?v=9ECqL51SRUk**)

CALL: Drop the coin right into the slot.
RESPONSE: (Guitar riff)
CALL: You gotta get something that's really hot.
RESPONSE: (Guitar riff)

Using Call and Response to Write a Blues Song

Simply think of a phrase in your head and then put musical notes to it. For example, I wrote an arrangement (featured soon below) based on a phrase, "The Blues had a baby and they called it Rock and Roll", from some song I must have heard when I was a teenager. I used the phrase in the song as a "call" and then added a "response" to it. Now that's quite a long phrase (2 bars and 1 beat) and for your first song it might be easier to pick a shorter phrase (only one bar = 4 beats in length).

Think of the main words falling on the beat as you clap your hands 4 times. Here are some more examples of call and response:

&	1	&	2	&	3	&	4	&	1
			Ba-	by	please		Don't		go
		She	Got		Dim	Ples	On	Her	chin
			Boom		Boom		Boom		boom
I'm your	Hoo-	Chie	Coo-	Chie	Man				
		Fur-	Ther	On		Up	The	road	

Note: some of these phrases start before the 1st beat, this is known as a **pickup note** (- you're "picking up" the tune early).

Exercise 1:
Write your own blues songs. For inspiration, listen to some more songs that use the Call and Response technique (often a sung phrase followed by a guitar riff), for example: Muddy Waters, **Hoochie Coochie Man**; or John Lee Hooker, **Boom, Boom; Dimples**

Exercise 2:
Here is a classic 8 bar blues song in the key of G minor. There are many covers, but versions by Lightnin' Hopkins, Seasick Steve, and Muddy Waters spring to mind. This version for the ukulele is different, a little jazzier, as it is inspired by Mickey Baker from an album I bought as a kid called: Mickey Baker, **Blues and Jazz Guitar** on Stefan Grossman's **Kicking Mule Records** label.

Baby Please Don't Go (4/4)

|Gm |Gm | Gm | Gm |
|Cm7 |D7 | Gm | Gm |

Baby please don't [Gm] go
Baby please don't go
Baby please don't [Cm7] go
Back to [D7] New Orleans
Because I [Gm] love you so

Turn your lamp down low x3
Baby please don't go
Because I love you so

Woman how you sound x3
You treat me like a clown
You're givin' me the messin' around

Got me way down here x3
You got me walkin' along
You treat me like a dog

Baby Please Don't Go (chord melody)

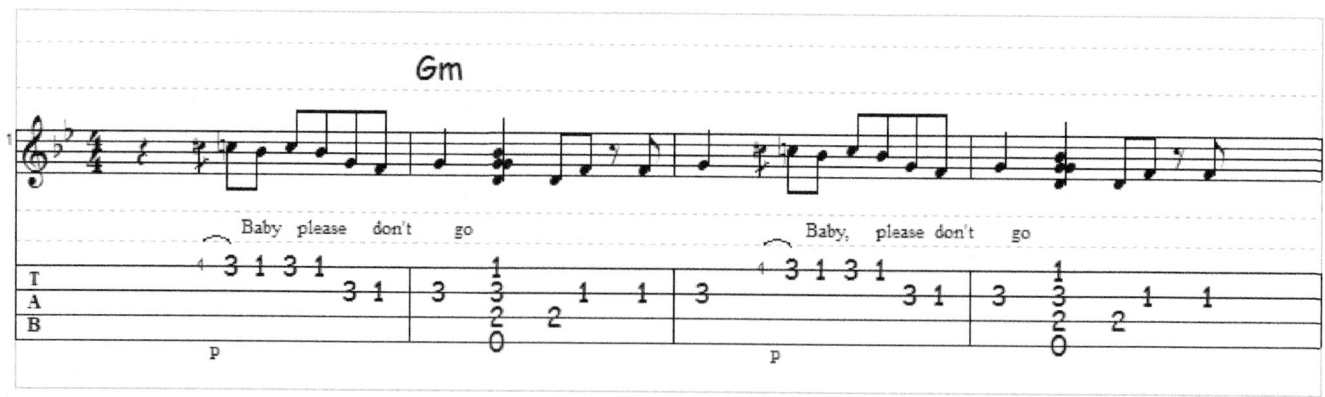

Notes:
A quick pull-off note begins the "call" phrase in Gm. The "response" phrase occurs in bars 2 and 4. Also, Cm7 is a new chord shape: easily played by barring across all the strings at fret 3. The root of this chord is on the 1st string, 3rd fret.

Improvising

Record the song as a backing track and try improvising using the ideas from previous lessons:

1. Learn the melody by heart
2. Play just the arpeggios (the notes of the chords) over each chord change
3. Use the G blues scale (given below) but only play quarter notes (or use some other rhythmic limitation)
4. Finally, freely improvise using the G blues scale

G Blues Scale (notes: G Bb C C# D F)

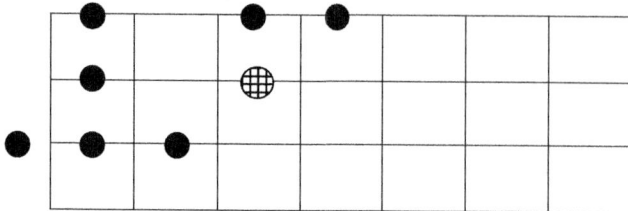

G Blues Scale (root at 3rd fret)

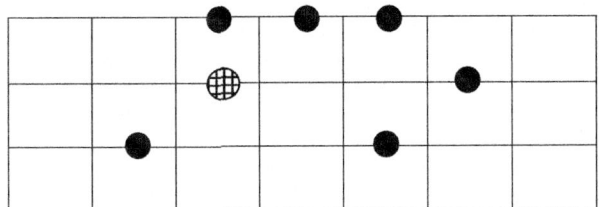

Here is music and TAB for both patterns (start and end on the root note G to orientate your ear):

LESSON 18
Right hand fingerpicking patterns - syncopation - Call and Response

Strumming is great but fingerpicking adds a whole new dimension to your playing. The exercises in this lesson help build technique so that you can keep a steady pulse with the thumb while picking out melody notes with the other fingers. Exercises 6 and 7 introduce **syncopation** (playing off the beat).

Right hand fingerpicking – one approach

Place right hand fingers on one string: p (thumb) on 4th string; i on 3rd string; m on 2nd string; a on 1st string. The fingers never stray from these strings. Even if there are two or three notes played in succession on the 1st string, the 'a' finger plays them all. Here are some exercises to get used to this approach:

Exercise 1: Thumb and ring finger (p & a) 'pinch' together

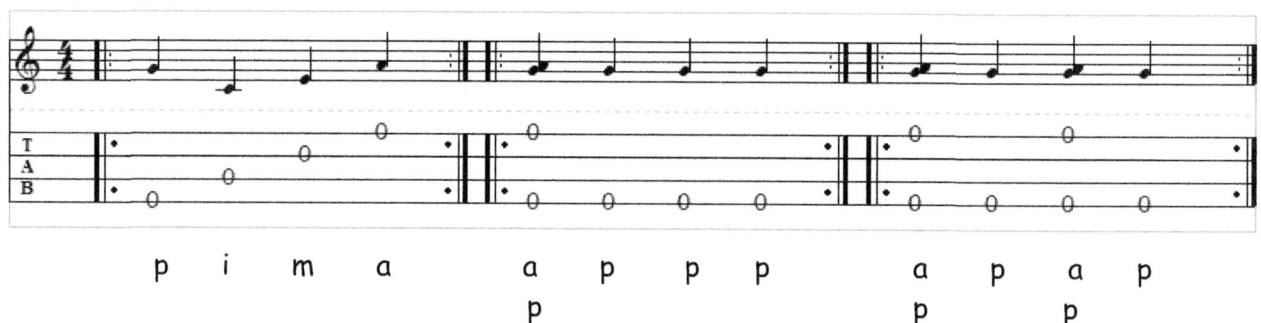

Exercise 2: Thumb and middle finger (p & m) 'pinch' together

Exercise 3: Thumb and index finger (p & i) 'pinch' together

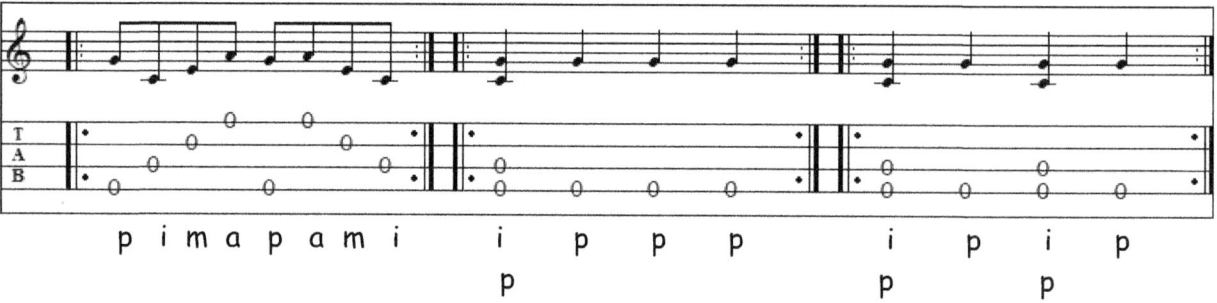

Exercise 4: The pinch on every beat

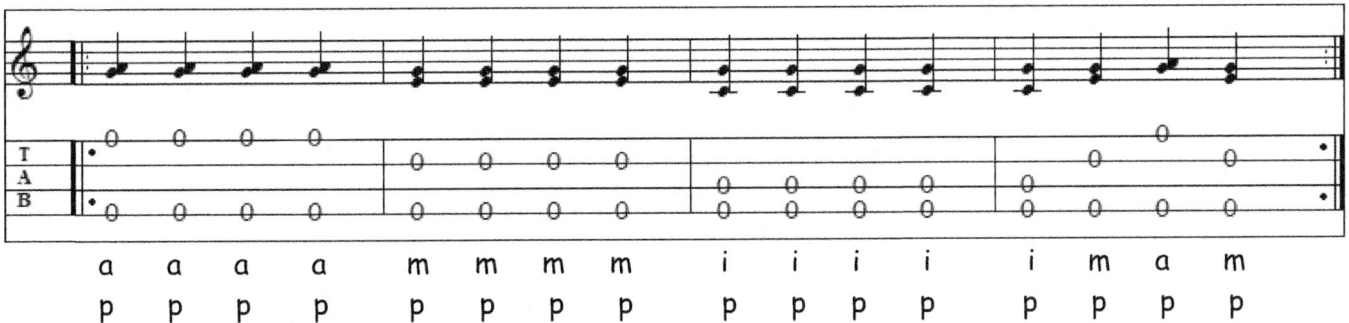

Exercise 5: The C Blues Scale with pinch

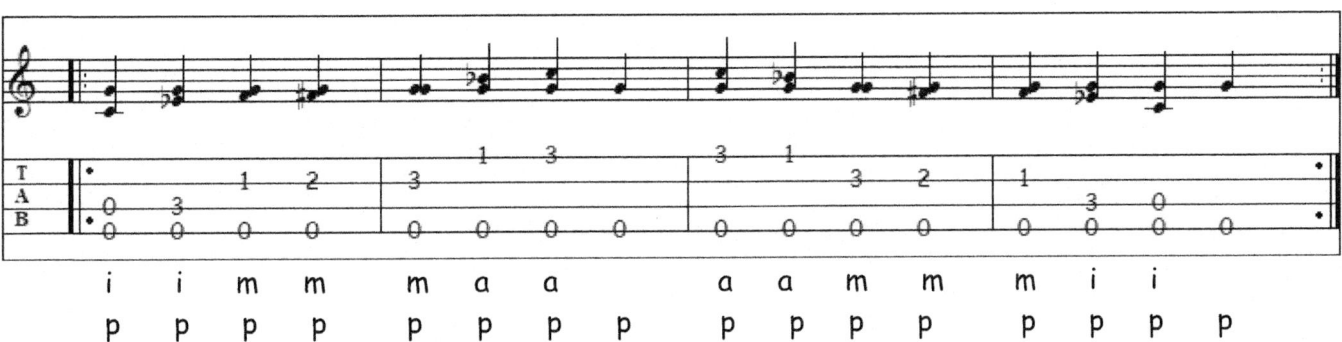

Exercise 6: Syncopation

To create more rhythmic interest we use **syncopation** which means playing and sometimes stressing the off beats. In the example above we play a steady 4 beat, on the beat, pulse with the thumb (counting 1, 2, 3, 4 with every thumb beat), then adding the open 1st string on the off-beat (the "&" between the beats). Play all the 1st string notes with the ring finger (a).
Repeat the same pattern using the m finger on the 2nd string.
Repeat the same pattern using the i finger on the 3rd string.

Exercise 7: Syncopation with melody notes

Keep the fingers on their designated string: i.e. the 'a' finger plays all the notes on the 1st string; the 'm' finger plays all the notes on the 2nd string and the 'I' finger plays all the notes on the 3rd string. The first two bars are a "call and response" over the C chord. The final bar is the "response" used in the next tune, so practise it until it feels comfortable and then the following tune will be fairly straightforward to play.

There is a song with various versions (one by Muddy Waters) which is called, **The Blues had a Baby (and they called it Rock and Roll)** but mine is from a vague and distant memory of that song (all I remembered was the title) and bears little, if any, resemblance. It does, however, illustrate the **call and response** technique. It also shows how you can turn a short phrase into a melody (expressed in bars 1 and 2), then add another phrase in response (bars 3 and 4). Sometimes **call and response** is named **question and answer** but, either way, you are creating a musical conversation.

The Blues Had a Baby

Performance Notes:
Fingerpicking is used here as opposed to strumming.
1. Use the thumb only on the 4th string to play the steady 4 beat pulse drone notes (G mostly with A on the F7 chords)
2. Use either a, m and i on the 1st, 2nd and 3rd strings respectively to play the melody (as in the 7 Exercises); or just use i and m to play the melody notes on the 1st and 2nd string, then the 2nd and 3rd string – both methods are acceptable and widely used.

Let's analyse the above music, with special reference to **"call and response"**:

1. There is a steady **drone bass** on the 4th string. It is a G for both C and G7 and this works because G is the 5th of C and the root note of G7. For the F7 chord, the note A is played on the 4th string and this works because A is the 3rd of F7. Ideally, we would use the root note of the chord as the bass (or on the lowest string) so that would mean the note C for the C chord, F for the F7 chord and G for the G7 chord. We could and probably would do that on guitar. However, because of the ukulele's limitations (only 4 strings) we have to go for the next best thing: a note that is in the chord. Also, because the 4th string is "re-entrant": i.e. tuned an octave higher than we would expect, it has an unexpected chiming quality – but that is all part of the ukulele's charm.
2. The call is a long one, lasting two bars and 1 beat (9 beats in total).
The first bar melody notes (played on strings 1 and 2) are from the phrase in my head: "Blues had a ba-by" (5 syllables, so 5 notes).
The second bar melody (on strings 2 and 3) is "called it rock and…" (4 syllables – 4 notes).
The melody ends on the first beat of the third bar (the open 3rd string): "…roll."
3. What follows in bar 3 is the response, and it is repeated in bar 4.
4. Bar 5 is "Blues had a baby" on the F7 chord, repeated in bar 6. Then the same response in bars 3 and 4 is repeated in bars 7 and 8.
5. Bars 9 and 10 vary the melody.
6. Bar 11 repeats the "response" exactly as bars 3, 4, 7 and 8.
7. Bar 12 is a "turnaround" on G7 to get us back to the beginning of the song.

LESSON 19
Fingerpicking THE BLUES IN Gm - You Got to Move

This is a great, hypnotic blues featured on Mississippi Fred McDowell's, **This Ain't No Rock'n'Roll** and on The Rolling Stones, **Sticky Fingers** album.

You Got To Move (4/4)

| Gm | Gm | C7 | Gm |
| Gm | D7 | Gm | Gm |

You got to [Gm] move
You got to move
You got to [C7] move, child
You got to [Gm] move
Oh, when the Lord gets [D7] ready
You got to [Gm] move

You may be [Gm] high
You may be low
You may be [C7] rich, child
You may be [Gm] poor
But when the lord gets [D7] ready
You got to [Gm] move

You see that [Gm] woman
Who walks the street
You see that [C7] police
Upon his [Gm] beat
But then the lord gets [D7] ready
You got to [Gm] move

You got to move

Note: you can alternate the sung verses above with my solo arrangement below. My arrangement might be quite tricky to play. Let's break it down. First learn the repeated riff:

1. Next, the easiest way to learn a tricky piece is to start by learning just the melody:

Notes:
- Right hand fingering is a matter of choice – use any combination of i m and a that feels comfortable (just remember to keep the thumb on the 4th string because in the full version it will be playing a steady 4 beat pulse there).
- Left hand fingering: 2nd position – i.e. finger 1 on the 2nd fret; finger 2 on the 3rd fret, etc…
- Bar 6 is best played by stretching finger 4 up to the 6th fret, while remaining anchored on the 2nd fret and 3rd frets with your 1st finger and 2nd fingers.
- N.B. Although the key signature has two flats, Bb and Eb, there are no E's in the melody and the B is played naturally except for bar 6 where it is Bb. The melody shows the ambiguity of the blues as it has both major and minor sound (B is the third of G major; but Bb is the third of G minor).

2. Once you are comfortable with the melody you could add a steady thumb pulse on the fourth string in preparation for the full version below:

You Got To Move

The hypnotic 4th string thumb beat is a great technique to learn (see lessons on "the Drone" in Book 2) and you can apply it to many different styles of music, not just the blues. However, sometimes the blues can benefit from a more "loose" approach. In the next arrangement of the same song, I've dispensed with the regular thumb beat and used more space, using just the G5 chord (neither major nor minor as there is no third) to keep a groove going, for a looser, more relaxed style:

You Got To Move ('groove' version)

LESSON 20
The Riff – Little Red Rooster (Key C)

Another classic blues song, recorded by Howlin' Wolf and The Rolling Stones among others. A **riff** is a short, repeated phrase and this song is a perfect example of a call and response blues riff.

LITTLE RED ROOSTER (4/4)

Intro Riff: play notes C F Eb C *(on 3rd string)* then slide up to
   C on 2nd string, 8th fret x4

F7	F7	C riff	C riff
F7	F7	C riff	C riff
G7	F7	C riff	C riff

[F7] I am the little red rooster, too lazy to crow for day,
riff x2
[F7] I am the little red rooster, too lazy to crow for day.
[G] Keep everything in the farm yard
[F7] upset in every way.
Riff x2

[F7] The dogs begin to bark and hounds begin to howl.
Riff x2
[F7] Dogs begin to bark and hounds begin to howl.
[G] Watch out strange cat people,
[F7] little red rooster's on the prowl.
Riff x2

[F7] If you see my little red rooster, please drive him home.
Riff x2
[F7] If you see my little red rooster, please drive him home.
[G] Ain't had no peace in the farm yard,
[F7] since my little red rooster's been gone.
Riff x2

Note: If you wish to play along with a recording then The Rolling Stones version is in the Key of G (G riff: C Bb G g ; chords: C7, G riff; C7, G riff; D7, C7, G riff); and Howlin' Wolf plays the song in the Key of A (A riff: D C A a; chords: D7, A riff; D7 A riff; E7, D7, A riff)

The Riff (in the Key of C)

The riff (C F Eb C) is played on the 3rd string of the ukulele (see bars 1 and 2). Bar 3 is the same riff but adding notes a third above (on the 2nd string).

The 4th bar adds the high C note on the 8th fret of the 2nd string, which is effective if slid up to from a lower fret (sliding up from the 5th fret feels comfortable). It is easier to play the C on the 1st string 3rd fret but the same note on the 2nd string, 8th fret is more effective because you can slide into then bend the note more easily.

What follows is a 'bare bones' chord melody arrangement, add extra strumming according to taste.

First, practise the riff in isolation as it is the most difficult part of the arrangement.

Little Red Rooster (solo arrangement)

Performance notes:
One of my favourite arrangements, and has a great groove.
Watch the repeat signs.
Play loose and relaxed and remember the slide on the 2nd string.
Two variations given – melody at the nut and then, second time through, higher up the neck.

LESSON 21
Blues in A - I'm So Glad

I'm So Glad by Skip James

The English musicians in the 60's were greatly influenced by the black blues musicians in America and "supergroup" Cream reworked many classic blues songs: **Rollin' and Tumblin'; Spoonful, Born Under a Bad Sign;** Robert Johnson's **Crossroads;** and this one, **I'm So Glad** by Skip James.

The song is characterised by a half-step (semitone) descending chord progression. The A chord shape is moved up to the 4th fret and descends a fret every bar until it is back to the 1st fret (so the A shape makes the chords Db, C, B, Bb, A). The pmpi fingerpicking pattern is repeated for all chords. In the original Skip James version a different pattern is used, likewise in the Cream version, but this pattern is effective on the ukulele.

Intro/riff:

I'm So Glad (4/4)

```
Intro/riff (as above):  | Db  | C   | B    | Bb  | A   | x2
Chorus:                 | A   | G   | A G  | A   | x2
Verse:                  | A   | Bm  | C Bm | A   | x2
```

CHORUS: [A] I'm so glad, [G] I'm so glad
I'm [A] glad, I'm [G] glad, I'm [A] glad
I'm so glad, [G] I'm so glad
I'm [A] glad, I'm [G] glad, I'm [A] glad

VERSE: I don't know what to do, I [Bm] don't know what to do,
I [C] don't know [Bm] what to [A] do
I'm tired of weeping, I'm [Bm] tired of moaning,
I'm [C] tired of [Bm] crying for [A] you

CHORUS: I'm so glad...

VERSE: I'm tired of weeping, I'm tired of moaning,
I'm tired of groaning for you
I don't know what to do, I don't know what to do,
I don't know what to do

REPEAT CHORUS then REPEAT INTRO

IMPROVISING: Use the A Blues Scale (from Lesson 12) over the **Chorus** chord progression.

PART FOUR
TWO MORE CLASSIC BLUES IN C AND Dm
The Five Blues Scale Patterns

LESSON 22
More fingerpicking in C - Tin Roof Blues

Here is another piece in C, based on a **riff** from an old (1923) jazz/blues instrumental called **Tin Roof Blues** which has a catchy melody which descends a half step (semitone) at a time. The **"layover"** technique is used here (see **Performance notes** below).

Tin Roof Blues

Performance notes:
1. Thumb plays a steady 4 beat to the bar rhythm but on different strings (use the thumb for all "steady bass" notes, including the F note on the 2nd string in bars 5 and 6)
2. There are too many notes and they happen too fast for one finger to play them all as in the previous blues tunes. So, this time we have to use the alternating i and m fingers to play the melody.
3. The F chord, uses a **"layover"** (the 1st finger makes a small barre from 2nd string 1st fret to 1st string 1st fret) so that the bass and melody can be played together (bar 5, 2nd beat)
4. A **"turnaround"** completes the song in the last two bars

LESSON 23
Key of Dm - Saint James Infirmary

To conclude this book, here is another early blues song that blurs the boundaries between jazz and blues. There are many wonderful versions – Cab Calloway, Arlo Guthrie, Louis Armstrong and, more recently, Stephen Laurie of House fame in his first solo album, **Let Them Talk.**

I used to play in a band called The Savannah Street Stompers (a bit of a flash name for a band based in the north of England but, why not?) and this was one of our favourites – it's on YouTube somewhere. Also, you might want to check out the Louis Armstrong version here:
https://www.youtube.com/watch?v=QzcpUdBw7gs
For the last bar I like to use A7#9 (known in rock music as 'The Hendrix chord' as Jimi Hendrix used it a lot: e.g. on **Foxy Lady** and **Stone Free**):

A7#9

Also, as with most old songs, there are many different lyrics, but here is a composite of my favourites:

Saint James Infirmary

| Dm A7 | Dm | Dm Gm | A7 |
| Dm A7 | Dm | Bb7 A7 | Dm A7#9 |

It was [Dm] down in [A7] Old Joe's [Dm] barroom,
At the corner [Gm] by the [A7] square;
The [Dm] drinks were [A7] served as [Dm] usual,
And the [Bb7] usual [A7] crowd was [Dm] there. [A7#9]

On my left stood Big Joe McKenny,
His eyes bloodshot and red,
He gazed at the crowd around him,
And these were the words he said:

"I went down to the St. James Infirmary,
I saw my baby there,
stretched out on a long, white table,
So young, so cold, so fair."

Let her go, let her go, God bless her,
Wherever she may be
She can search this whole wide world over
She won't ever find another man like me

"Sixteen coal-black horses,
Hitched to a rubber-tired hack,
Carried seven girls to the graveyard,
Only six of 'em came back."

Now when I die,
Bury me in straight lace shoes
A box back coat and a Stetson hat
Put a twenty dollar gold piece on my watch chain,
So the boys'll know I died standin' pat

Six poker dealers for pall bearers,
Let a whore sing my funeral song,
With a red hot band just beatin it out
Raisin hell as we roll along

Folks, now that you have heard my story,
Say, boy, hand me another shot of that booze;
If anyone should ask you, Tell 'em
I've got those St. James Infirmary blues.

St James Infirmary (melody)

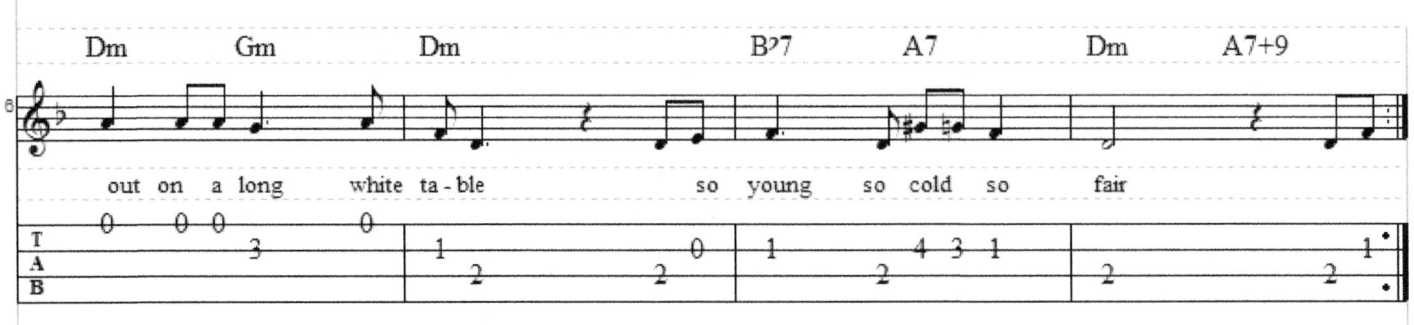

St James Infirmary (chord melody)

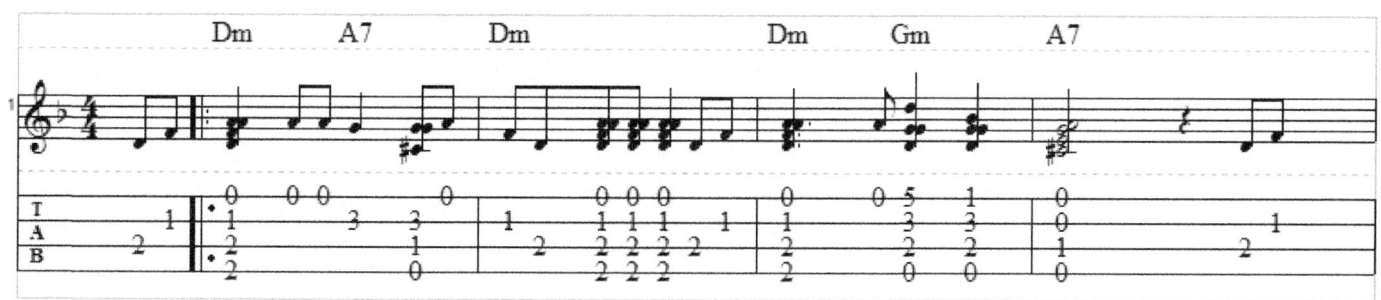

Improvising

For this song use the **D Blues Scale** – the two patterns below cover the first five frets.

D Blues Scale (D F G G# A C)

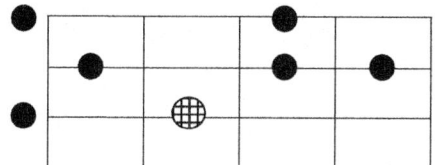
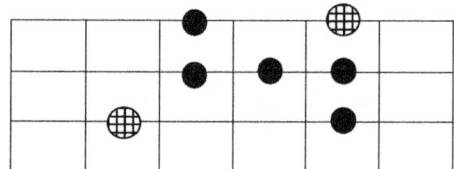

IMPROVISING TIPS

1. Learn the melody and play it over a backing track of the chords
2. Play only the root note of every chord along with the backing track
3. Play only the arpeggio of every chord along with the backing track
4. Play along using the Blues Scale

LESSON 24

PUTTING IT ALL TOGETHER

Everything you need is on the very next page – it really is a page to print out and put on your wall, a page to work with to unlock the magic of your ukulele fretboard.

Here is the explanation.

COLUMN 1: BLUES SCALE
This shows every Blues Scale in the Key of C – starting at the nut, then fret 3, fret 5 and so on until the whole 12 fret fingerboard is covered. If you have more frets then the patterns just repeat. The roots (the note C) are all shown by the checked circle so the patterns are all moveable. For example, if we take the second pattern (beginning at fret 3) then the root is on the 1st string. Move it up to fret 5 and you get the D Blues Scale; move it to fret 7 and you get the E blues scale.

COLUMN 2: MAJOR CHORD SHAPE
This column shows every C Major chord shape that fits with the Blues scale in column 1. So that, with practice whenever you play that shape for a chord, you will know the Blues scale that fits around it. Again, the shapes are all moveable, just use the root to identify the name of the chord.

COLUMN 3: MINOR CHORD SHAPE
This shows every C Minor chord shape that corresponds with the Blues scale in the same row.

COLUMN 3: 7th CHORD SHAPE
This shows every C7 chord shape and the same points given above apply. Note that, the shapes in the first and fifth rows are the same. The difference is that you would play the first shape by barring with the 1st finger (except for C7 shown here, because it uses the nut – however, when you move it up the fretboard your 1st finger takes over the job). The 7th chord shape in the last row is best barred with your 3rd finger, with your pinkie playing the note on the 1st string (which frees up your 1st and 2nd fingers for the Blues scale in that row).

You might have to read this page a few times if it is all new to you but this Lesson puts it all together and gives you a framework to play Blues all over the fretboard; you just need to work on the next page until it is in your memory. It is best to learn the scales in the order shown as, once familiar, you can run one scale into another.

Suggested Procedure

1. Pick a Key (e.g. C)
2. Start with row 1: learn the C major chord shape and the C Blues Scale at the nut.
3. Record a I IV V7 (C F G7) blues progression (three 12 Bar progressions are given in Lesson 5) and improvise using your first Blues scale pattern.
4. Next, row 2: learn the second Blues scale pattern (at fret 3) and the corresponding C major chord and use only that scale to improvise.
5. Try running the first two Blues patterns together.

    Repeat the above steps for the third, fourth and fifth Blues Scale patterns.
    Then, try improvising over the minor chords (Cm Fm Gm or G7), or the 7ths (C7 F7 G7); or pick another key and follow the same 5 step procedure.

The Blues Scale (the Five Patterns)

BLUES SCALE	MAJOR CHORD SHAPE	MINOR CHORD SHAPE	7th CHORD SHAPE

AFTERWORD

My goal, In this series of 4 books, is to build a comprehensive library of songs and techniques for the ukulele – a complete method.

In Book 3, we focused on classic Blues songs, covering:

- 12 Bar and 8 Bar Blues structures
- Major and minor Keys: C F A Gm Dm
- Turnarounds
- Improvising using Blues Scales in C, A, G and D
- The Blues shuffle
- The Flamenco strum (not strictly blues, but flamenco is another great improvised music and the strum sounds so good on **Sitting on Top of the World** I had to put it in)
- The Nashville and Classical number systems and Transposing
- Bends and vibrato
- Licks mixing major and minor 3rds
- Fingerpicking
- Call and Response
- Writing Blues

I love the blues and feel it is unmatched for deep feeling and expression. For my money, some old blues men can create more music with one chord than a whole orchestra of classical musicians playing a symphony. The Blues has profound depth and subtlety and I hope this book has given you pleasure and a little insight into what a powerful art form the Blues is.

Videos to support this and my other ukulele books can be found by typing, "Ukulele Beginner to Brilliant" into the YouTube search box or using this link here and then selecting the appropriate "Playlist" (e.g. "Book 3"):

https://www.youtube.com/channel/UCHY9Vic35cnPiN8uHyaKZcw/playlists

The final book in this "complete method", Book 4: Advanced, discusses the problems I've encountered learning music and presents you with a SYSTEM that turns the whole world of music into something simple, graspable and practical. It is the final part of the puzzle where I provide solutions for the ukulele player who has reached a reasonable technical level but feels stuck in their understanding of music and wants to develop into a complete musician, able to play by ear and improvise.

Happy playing,
Doug

Appendix

The Cycle of Fifths Explained

Cycle of Fifths

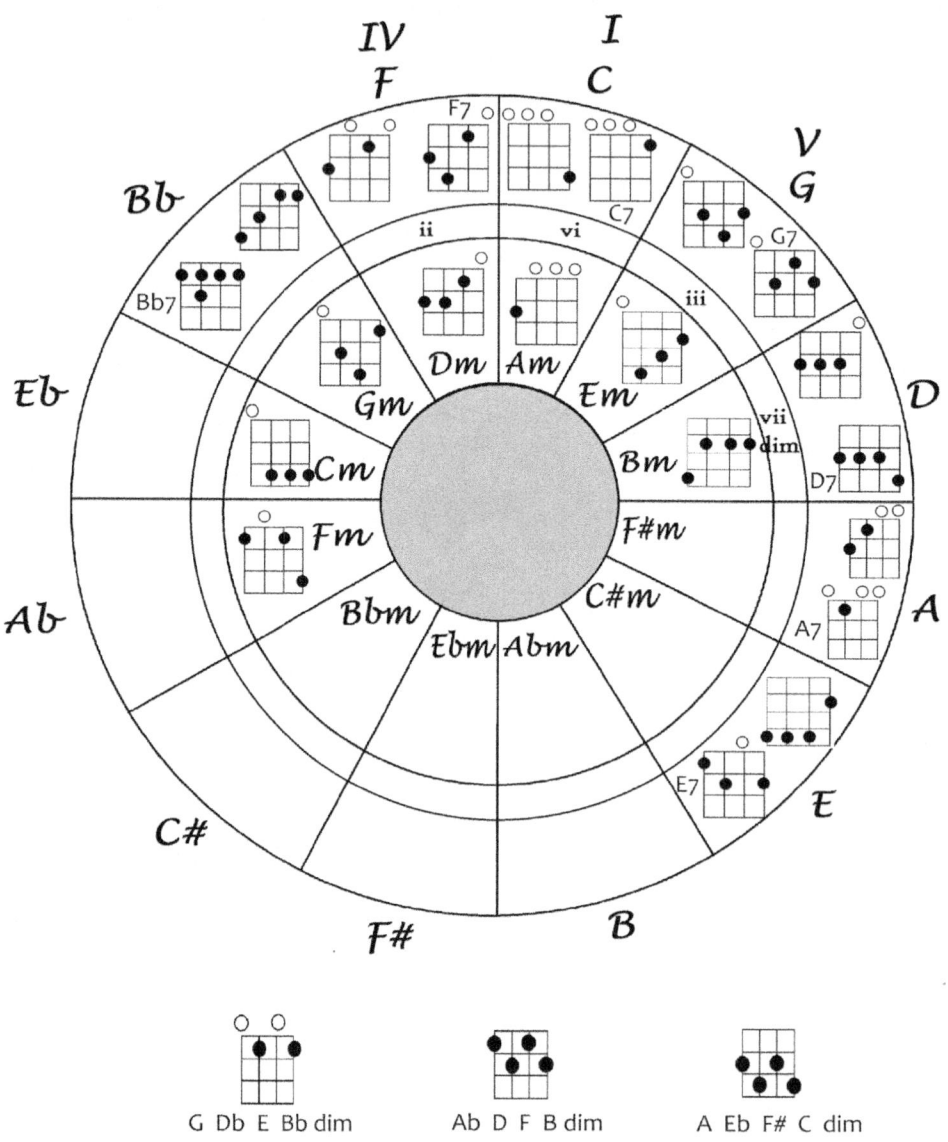

If we go clockwise round the circle we see the notes go up by intervals of a fifth: i.e. at the top right we have C, then G (if we name the notes – C D E F G – numbering C as note 1 then G is the 5th note in the sequence so we call that interval a 5th). The next note is D which is a 5th above G (G A B C D), and so on around the cycle until we return to C.

Above C is the Roman numeral I. Above G is the Roman numeral V. Above F - IV.

This gives us the I IV V chords in the key of C: C F and G.

The inner ring gives us the relative minors. So, if we look at the C segment, the inner ring gives us the chord A minor (Am), which is the vi (the sixth degree of the C major scale). To the left is Dm (built on the 2nd degree of the C major scale) and to the right is the iii chord, Em (built on the 3rd degree of the C major scale. Finally, we have the vii diminished chord (which would be B diminished). The diminished chord only has one shape (for all 12 chords) so it is shown below the cycle to avoid confusion.

Simply put the Roman numerals are the standard way of notating the different chords and here we have the whole key of C: C, Dm, Em, F, G, Am, Bdim.

So, what do we do with it?

Well, two things.

First it shows you what chords are available in the key of C.

Second, it shows you what chords are available in all the keys. So, if you want to transpose a song from the key of C to the key of G then you would imagine the numbers are on dials and twist them one step to the right so G now becomes your I chord. That makes C the IV chord, D the V chord and Em the vi chord.

The blank segments are the less common keys but, for a ukulele player, you can play these chords by moving the chords you already know up or down. For example, to play C# just move your C shape up, replacing the nut with the 1st finger barring at the 1st fret. For Eb, just move your E shape down one fret.

ABOUT THE AUTHOR

Doug started playing the guitar at 13 and was in a jazz band in his twenties. His love affair with the ukulele began because he couldn't bear to go on holiday without something he could play a tune on and the soprano ukulele fitted nicely into his airplane hand luggage. It was also easy to throw in a car, and when he'd take his young children to the park to go on the climbing frames, swings and slides, he would sit on a bench and strum his favourite songs. No one seemed to mind and he didn't get arrested.

Also, he used to teach English in schools and colleges, but he managed to escape.

Printed in Great Britain
by Amazon